18565

D1108261

Library
Oakland S.U.M.

18565

Library
Oakland S,U.M.

FIRST UNITED PRESBYTERIAN CHURCH
2619 BROADWAY
OAKLAND 12, CALIFORNIA

YOU SHALL BE MY PEOPLE

The Books of Covenant and Law

WESTMINSTER GUIDES TO THE BIBLE

Edwin M. Good, General Editor

YOU
SHALL BE
MY PEOPLE

The Books of Covenant and Law

EDWIN M. GOOD

Philadelphia
THE WESTMINSTER PRESS

© W. L. JENKINS MCMLIX

All rights reserved — no part of this book may be reproduced in any form without permission in writing from the publisher, except by a reviewer who wishes to quote brief passages in connection with a review in magazine or newspaper.

Scripture quotations from the Revised Standard Version of the Bible are copyright, 1946 and 1952, by the Division of Christian Education of the National Council of Churches, and are used by permission.

LIBRARY OF CONGRESS CATALOG CARD NO. 59–5341

PRINTED IN THE UNITED STATES OF AMERICA

Contents

1906

Preface

Perhaps the books of Genesis through Deuteronomy have proved the downfall of innumerable resolutions to read the Bible from beginning to end. But this book is written in the confidence that the difficulties are worth surmounting. The vistas of faith that open to us from the narratives of Moses, of Abraham, Isaac, and Jacob; the penetrating self-understanding of the stories of Creation, of Adam and Eve, of Noah; the depth of devotion behind the law; the grand vision of God enshrined in even the " begats," are of burning significance to Christians. For these five books stand at the base of Old Testament faith. And though we think most often of the prophets as the spiritual ancestors of Jesus and the church, the Pentateuch played its very important role as Scripture for the earliest Christians.

I have tried to center the interpretation around the community of faith. The meanings of the various kinds of stories and of the parts of the Pentateuch are to be found in the meanings they had to those who told the stories and preserved them as the voice of God to and through his people. We must start here if the Pentateuch is to become meaningful to us. When we see the meanings that these stories had for Israel as she heard and told them through the centuries, we may then go on to see what they mean to us. We shall find the Israelite community the true ancestor of our Christian community.

The Westminster Guides to the Bible grew in the first instance out of the stimulus of the Layman's Theological Library. If, we thought, laymen in the church could be so eloquently encouraged to be theologians, why could they not be encouraged to be Bible scholars as well? In the modern resurgence of serious thinking about the Christian faith, the study of the Bible has played a major role. But the methods and results of this recent study have not been made available to laymen.

The Westminster Guides to the Bible seek to fill this gap. In nine brief volumes, we introduce the riches of the major portions of the Bible and of the period " between the Testaments." The writers share the conviction that the Bible lies at the heart of Christianity, and that it is imperative that laymen be aided to take a firm grip on Biblical faith. We are certain that this means no denial of the mind. On the contrary, the Bible demands the utmost our minds can give it, and searching study repays our efforts with new insight.

Of course, we are primarily concerned with the Bible, not with our books about it. We hope that the reader will have his Bible in hand as he reads these books, and that he will turn to it again with greater anticipation when he has finished.

And it is with laymen, who are the backbone of the church, that we are concerned. We have written, not for scholars already learned, but for those who seek to learn. We are certain that no wishy-washy faith, no cheap " religiousness," is wanted. In the vigor of Biblical faith we trust that the reader will find invigoration. If so, the church of Christ will be served.

EDWIN M. GOOD

CHAPTER 1 | *An Answer to God*

GOD speaks to men. Everything the Bible says about God develops this theme. Although God sometimes speaks in words, he usually speaks by actions. We often say that people can be known better by what they do than by what they say. We speak more eloquently by one deed of love than by many books written about love. So God speaks to men. He tells us most clearly what we need to know by what he does to us.

To this the Bible consistently testifies. The men of the Bible heard God speaking first of all in what he did. In certain great events he had spoken to the people Israel, spoken so clearly that they could not doubt the reality of his acting. And whenever they recounted the story of one of those events, the speech of God came through again. Even those who had not experienced the original event heard God's voice in the story.

This means, of course, that when God speaks, men must answer. They must sit up, take notice, and say yes when he acts. They must obey a clear command, they must remember a significant occurrence, they must go on the way that God points to them. From then on they tell the story. Telling the story itself is an answer to God, for the men of the Bible remembered the events of God's history not because the stories were entertaining but because God had spoken. Whenever

9

they told the story and remembered the event again, they were responding to what God had done and what he had said.

In this book we shall consider their response. The stories in the Pentateuch (the books of Genesis through Deuteronomy) recount the events that the people Israel considered most important. They remembered these particularly significant happenings much as we remember such solemn moments in history as the Reformation, the Declaration of Independence, or the Battle of Gettysburg.

The word " Pentateuch " tells us nothing more than that in ancient times five scrolls (in Greek, *penta,* five, and *teuchos,* scroll) were needed to contain these books. Sometimes the Pentateuch is called the " Five Books of Moses," which is also self-explanatory: there are five books here that tradition says were written by Moses. The Jews, however, call the first five books of the Bible the " Torah," which is a more profound description. It may be helpful if we take the Hebrew word *tōrāh* as a clue and key to what we may expect to find in the Pentateuch. *Tōrāh* has four main meanings: it sometimes means revelation (God's teaching); it sometimes means instruction (the teaching that men do); it often means law; and occasionally it is something very close to wisdom. Let us look at these in order.

God Acts

When Israel wanted to know God, she looked not to nature but to history, not to the stars and the sunsets but to the events of the past and of the present. Israel understood her experience in history to be the medium through which God spoke to her of himself. God acted so that men might know him. The Pentateuch is the Torah, that is, it tells of that history in which God revealed himself.

This is not " any old history." It is Israel's history. God is found to be at work in *certain* events. Through particular acts, he speaks to men. The Torah does not even pretend to tell everything that happened from the Creation to Moses' death. It tells only those occurrences in which the people Israel heard God's word to them. For God always acts in accord with his people's need: what he does is intended to strengthen their commitment to him. Sometimes he acts benevolently in order to preserve them. At other times he punishes them in order that they might return to their faith. The history of which the Torah speaks, however, was always the primary source for Israel's relationship to God.

Israel looked first to the events that surrounded the exodus, when God delivered the people from Egypt and sent them through a long wandering in the wilderness. The very way in which Israel described the exodus shows that she saw God at work there. And when, at Mt. Sinai, God spoke to the people, pledging his faithfulness and demanding their responsive obedience, they gladly gave it. God had made a covenant with Israel. Israel was his people, and he was their God. They sometimes forgot, as when they made a calf to worship. They sometimes acted as if they would rather be free of God, as when they murmured about going back to Egypt where life had been easy. But God was faithful even when Israel was not.

Israel looked behind the exodus to the tales of the ancestors: Abraham, Isaac, Jacob, and Joseph. Abraham had been called out of his old home and sent off to the Land of Canaan not because he had a wanderlust but because God impelled him. And God promised that Abraham's descendants would possess this pleasant land. When Abraham objected that he had no descendants, God provided him with a son, Isaac, to whom the same promise was repeated: his descendants would possess the land. God continued the promise to Jacob, preserving him in all kinds of dangers, many of them brought on by Jacob's perverse tendency to do as he pleased. Joseph too was kept alive and brought to a position of high honor and responsibility, setting the stage for the Israelites to come to Egypt. Here and there, men had known that the hand of God was leading them through their experiences.

Israel looked behind even the patriarchs. Why is a covenant with Israel necessary? It is because men prefer to act as if God did not matter at all, as if they were gods themselves, directing their own affairs. If God is really God, he cannot countenance such an illusion. Expulsion from the delightful Garden kept Adam and Eve from trespassing on God's domain. A flood, a confusion of languages, prevented men from climbing higher than they should. But how was God to restore man to his lost and neglected manhood? If man of his own volition has rebelled against God, only God can bring him back. And Israel sees her covenant as the means by which God will reach all mankind. Israel's history reveals the God whom man needs to know, and the Torah, speaking of that history, speaks God's word to men. It is revelation.

ISRAEL TELLS THE STORY

Not all men have access to the experiences of one small nation. Is not Israel hopelessly narrow in claiming that God has acted in a special way in her particular history? So the objection runs. No Russian can understand the meaning of the American Revolution; nor can an American understand the Russian Revolution. It does not belong to him. It is not part of *his* history. In America, May Day is just another day. In Russia the Fourth of July has no significance. How, then, can anyone who is not a Jew understand the exodus as God's act?

We can carry this still farther. What about those later generations which were not present at the exodus? How could this event be made part of their own experience? How could they respond in obedience and trust to a God who had acted in the long past?

The second objection is easier to answer than the first. Though none of us was present on July 4, 1776, the Declaration of Independence is peculiarly ours. We have breathed the air of the nation so long that the nation's past is *our* past. The great men of United States history seem our familiar friends. So for the Jew with Moses and Abraham. The Jew lived as a Jew among other Jews and listened to the stories for so long that the events of the past became familiar and significant for him. He took them in and made them his own.

But a question is yet to be answered. How can a twentieth-century American understand the experience of an ancient, distant people? Israel would say to us: "Listen to the story; really listen to it. If God was speaking to us then, he speaks to us still in the story of the event." And it is true that through Israel's own story of the occurrences in which God spoke to her then, we hear God speaking to us now, if we only listen. The Torah is instruction. It tells us where to look to find God at work.

In its instruction, of course, the Torah does not merely tell a bare story. It indicates the conclusion to be drawn from the story. The events not only show us God's active presence, but they also tell us what is needful to know about God. Yet the people Israel never tried to put this information about God into abstract ideas. They never said that God is love, or that God is a spirit, or that God is omnipotent, or that God knows everything. If we were to ask them what God is like, they would answer by telling us the story of the exodus or of the Garden of Eden. They do not, in other words, have any "theology" as we use the term. We think of theology as a discussion about God, his character, his attributes, his relationship to man. Their "theology" consists in telling stories. If we are interested in ideas, we shall have to see what ideas the stories suggest to us. For the people Israel will do nothing for us except tell us what happened to them. That is the intention of the Torah. If we are willing to listen carefully and obediently to the stories, we shall learn of God from their instruction.

Israel Answers Yes

It is not enough, however, to hear entertaining stories. It is not enough to know about events. History is sometimes taught as if it were nothing but dates, names, and places. Why concern ourselves with something that happened long ago? What if God was there? Does that change anything?

The people Israel saw another dimension. God speaks and acts with a purpose. He does not come to Moses to overwhelm him with a miraculous bush that burns but is not burned up. "Come," he says, "I will send you to Pharaoh that you may bring forth my people, the sons of Israel, out of Egypt." (Ex. 3:10.) When God speaks, men must *do* something. God does not tell men what he wants so that they may nod their heads and say, "Yes, that's nice." He tells them so that they may say, "Yes, I will go and do what you say." God expects a response. "Hear, O Israel," is a continuous refrain in the Torah. And to hear is much more than to be aware that someone is talking. Hearing includes answering. When Israel hears, she acts in obedience. Indeed, the Hebrew word "to hear" is often rightly translated "to obey."

When the Egyptian army was swallowed up in the sea, and Israel stood safe on the east side, the people burst into song, according to the story:

"I will sing to the Lord, for he has triumphed gloriously;
    the horse and his rider he has thrown into the sea.

The Lord is my strength and my song,
   and he has become my salvation;
this is my God, and I will praise him,
   my father's God, and I will exalt him."

(Ex. 15:1-2.)

To God's act of deliverance, Israel answers yes. "This is my God, and I will praise him." Such an answer God wants. He expects his people to shoulder fidelity and obedience to him.

For " *tōrāh* " often means law, and law for the Hebrew people was the assurance of responsible life in obedience to God's command. There is a great deal of law in the Pentateuch. All of Leviticus, most of Deuteronomy, much of Numbers, and much of Exodus is made up of laws. We may wonder why we should bother with them. These are ancient laws, based on an order of society that is unfamiliar to us and impossible for us to enter. Many of the laws deal with ceremonies and sacrifices that have no real meaning for us today. Are we right to maintain these relics of a lost civilization in Holy Scripture? Can we refer to the ritual laws of Leviticus as God's word to us?

Clearly, in detail we cannot. Christians can hardly resume the practice of animal sacrifice for the forgiveness of sins. We know the forgiveness that comes through Christ, and no other will substitute for that, or even properly symbolize it. But we need to preserve the laws, for they remind us that God requires of us total obedience in every aspect of life. When man says yes to God, he says it with all his heart and soul and might (Deut. 6:5). He says it with his whole self. He must go and do what God requires. He must be " responsible " in the true sense of the word; he must " respond," answer God, with his whole life.

When God speaks, he speaks a command. When we answer, we answer with obedience. Not that God is an arbitrary tyrant. He acts in love for man's salvation. The central act of Israel's history is the exodus, an act that reveals a God of the most immense love. (See, for example, Ex. 19:4-6 and Deut. 7:6-8.) We love God in response, and that love is expressed in our joyful obedience. The Torah stands in Scripture as God's word, to remind us that life goes on from God's acts under a new compulsion. Israel said yes. The law is the manner in which Israel set about to act on that yes.

ISRAEL REFLECTS

We have already seen that when Israel tells the story of God's deeds, it turns out to be more than mere fact. The story incorporates in itself Israel's devout interpretation of what happened.

It is obvious, for example, that the historian, looking at the exodus, would write of it as nothing more than the escape of a subject people from a tyrannous Egypt. The circumstances were such that the Israelites could make their getaway. The reason they fled, the historian would have to say, was that they were being persecuted, and so wanted their freedom. The historian must interpret the facts in accordance with his method, and he could not allow that anything in the bare facts of the event demanded God's being in the picture. And he is right. If we had a motion picture of the exodus (despite Cecil B. DeMille, we have not!), it would show nothing more than what the historian says.

The Israelite knows that one cannot take pictures of God. (See Ex. 20:4.) But he would say: "Historian or no historian, God was there. This was no chance, that we escaped. God delivered us." There is an ingredient in the event, he would say, that is accessible only to faith. God's presence in the exodus cannot be proved to the person who doubts its possibility. It can only be affirmed by him who has heard God speak in the exodus story. The statement that God acts in history is not a statement of historic fact. We cannot demonstrate that it is so. It is, however, a confession of faith. We believe that it is so, for through those events we have heard God's voice in summons, in love, in command.

May we call this wisdom? *Tōrāh* sometimes has a meaning very close to that. The fact that the stories are told and the manner of their telling reveal to us that Israel has reflected long and hard on what God has done. As we read the moving story of Abraham's obedience to a command that he sacrifice his son Isaac (Gen., ch. 22), we discover depths of meaning, depths that reveal themselves to us one after the other, as if we were peeling back layer after layer and looking closer and closer to the heart of a people. What kind of God would command the sacrifice of a son? What kind of man would unquestioningly undertake it? The profundity of Abraham's response, the trust of the young lad Isaac, the sudden and dramatic discovery of the ram caught and struggling in the thicket, all speak of an insight into God's ways that has come with no little effort.

The ruthless honesty with which the storytellers probe their own people bespeaks the depth of their faith. The reflection of faith on history is no easy thing. Israel could not have found it pleasant to remember her own perversity as she heard the stories of Jacob, or to recall her obstinacy and faithlessness as she heard of the wandering in the wilderness, her sin as she listened to the stories of Adam, of Cain, of Noah. And let us make no mistake. These stories spoke not only of figures in the past but also of figures in Israel's present. Israel walks the pages of the Torah from beginning to end, and the portrait Israel paints of herself is a portrait without sham or illusion. We too walk about in these pages. They tell of our sin, of our faithlessness. They tell of our deliverance as well, though that whole story is not here.

But the portrait of man is only part of the picture. The real focus is on God. The God to whom Israel says yes occupies the center of the stage. What has happened is what he has done. The stories that are told are the stories of his deeds. The response of Israel in faithful obedience is a response to him. The reflection of faith is a reflection on his word to men. The Torah is from first to last a document wrought out of men's faith. And men's faith is wrought out of God's love.

CHAPTER 2 | *The Process of Memory*

In the first chapter, we sought to see what the Pentateuch is about, the purpose of its writing. Although we did not use the word in that chapter, the best description of this material might well be *memory*. Memory is supremely important for the religious life of the Bible. It is not merely idle recalling in a sentimental way. Memory is the recollection of what took place in the past as it speaks to us today. Thus, when we remember, we take the past into the present and we find that what happened " back there " sheds light on what we are doing " right here." To ask what God required of Israel in the past is really to ask what he requires of us now. When Israel remembered, the interest was focused not so much on the factual details of the past as it was on the meaning of past events. The books of the Torah are the deposit of Israel's memory of those pivotal events which told her that God was working his purposes through her.

In this chapter, we are interested principally in how and why these books came to be written. We shall watch the process of memory, seeing how the stories of the past spoke to many present moments, and how sometimes those moments spoke to the stories, altering them here, deepening them there. For the Pentateuch is the confession of a people's faith.

19

Though the faith does not change much, the confession
sometimes does.

SOME CURIOUS FACTS

Tradition says that the author of the Pentateuch was Moses.
The Pentateuch itself never claims to be written by Moses —
not that it is terribly important whether or not Moses wrote
it. But tradition dies hard, and we may preface our discussion
of the writing of the Pentateuch by noting some facts that
compel us to say that the tradition, for all its hoary age, is
mistaken. To note facts, of course, requires that we quote
chapter and verse, so that the facts may be verified.

In several places, the author of the Pentateuch has told the
same thing more than once. Twice, for example, God made a
covenant with Abraham that included the same promises
(Gen. 15:18 and ch. 17:2 ff.), although the second time the
command of circumcision was added. Two times Jacob's
name was changed from Jacob to Israel (Gen. 32:28 and
ch. 35:10), and twice Jacob renamed the town of Luz, Bethel
(Gen. 28:19 and ch. 35:15). Moses twice gave the Ten Commandments (Ex. 20:1-17 and Deut. 5:6-21) — offering two
different reasons for observing the Sabbath. Apparently six
times in the course of a year he commanded Sabbath observance as a general rule (Ex. 20:8-10; 23:12; 31:13-17; 34:21;
35:1-3; Lev. 23:3). On two occasions Abraham told rulers
whom he feared that Sarah, his wife, was really his sister (Gen.
12:10-20 and ch. 20); and Isaac, using the same victim, Abimelech, pulled the same trick with Rebekah (Gen. 26:6-11). (We
might think that Abimelech would learn after one such experience!)

Such duplications might not be so strange, but we find also
some rather odd inconsistencies of fact. When, for example,
we are asked how many animals Noah took into the ark, we

normally answer, two of each kind. If we read Gen. 6:19-20, we are right. If, however, we read ch. 7:2-3, we find the number to be seven pairs of clean animals and one pair of unclean ones. And what was the name of Moses' father-in-law? In Ex. 2:18 it is Reuel; in ch. 18:1, Jethro; and in Num. 10:29, apparently Hobab. Then there are the numbers. Numbers are easy to forget, indeed, but it is hard to see how Isaac, one hundred years old and on his deathbed (Gen. 27:1), could have blessed Jacob and then remained on his deathbed for eighty years, for he died at the age of one hundred and eighty (ch. 35:28). It is also difficult to understand how a nation that had been served adequately by two midwives (Ex. 1:15) should grow in a very few years to a population of 600,000 men plus women and children (ch. 12:37).

If these were the only examples, we might dismiss them. Another very interesting and somewhat crucial one may be noted, however. In translations of the Bible where the word "Lord" is spelled in large and small capital letters, the Hebrew text uses the word "Yahweh," the name of God. (See Chapter 3.) In Ex. 6:2-3, God says to Moses: "I am the LORD. I appeared to Abraham, to Isaac, and to Jacob, as God Almighty, but by my name the LORD I did not make myself known to them." Yet when we read Genesis, we find that Abraham, Isaac, and Jacob often refer to God as "Yahweh" ("the LORD").

These facts indicate simply that the writing of the Pentateuch was much more complicated than the tradition suggests. To try to bring order out of the complexity is a considerable task, and we must pass lightly over many debatable points.

AN ALPHABETIC PENTATEUCH

Most scholars have concluded that the Pentateuch is the interweaving of several basic writings into one connected story.

That is, at different times and places, the epic of Israel's beginning was written down. One account, so this theory goes,
was written very close to the time of David and Solomon. It
was a complete story of Israel from the Creation to the conquest of Canaan by Joshua (thus going beyond the Pentateuch). This document is called J, for in the book of Genesis it
consistently uses the term "Yahweh" (German scholars first
put forth this theory, and in German, "Yahweh" is spelled
"Jahweh"). Sometime later, it seems, after the division of the
nation into two kingdoms, another version of Israel's beginnings was written down in the Northern Kingdom. It began,
not with the Creation, but with Abraham, and because in Genesis it does not use God's name, Yahweh, but the word
"Elohim" (which means "God"), it is called E. These sym-
bols are a kind of shorthand to designate the origin of the
various passages that we now see combined in the Pentateuch.

At some time these two originally different epics were dovetailed, so that they made one story, which is called JE. Most
scholars think that this took place shortly after the destruction
of the Northern Kingdom in 721 B.C. About a century later
another document came to light, a lawbook, which, according
to II Kings, chs. 22 and 23, was the basis for King Josiah's
reformation in Judah. This book seems to have comprised
much of Deuteronomy, and it was perhaps combined with
the existing JE during the exile (586–538 B.C.). Deuteronomy,
of course, is called D, and its incorporation into JE produced
what we may call JED. A fourth document is also to be found,
a document that begins in Gen., ch. 1, with the Creation
and moves through the whole of the Pentateuch. The style of
this strand and its obvious interest in things that have to do
with priests and ritual show that it was written by priests, and
it is therefore designated as P. The organization of religion in
this document indicates that it came from the time after the

exile. When P was combined with JED, the result was the Pentateuch as we have it.

According to this Documentary Hypothesis (so called because it supposes that the Pentateuch is the result of the combination of written documents), at each stage of the process a job of editing was done. Those who did the editing are called redactors, and they may be designated by R. If we were to chart the theory, it would look something like this:

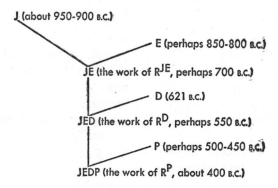

J (about 950-900 B.C.)

E (perhaps 850-800 B.C.)

JE (the work of R^{JE}, perhaps 700 B.C.)

D (621 B.C.)

JED (the work of R^D, perhaps 550 B.C.)

P (perhaps 500-450 B.C.)

JEDP (the work of R^P, about 400 B.C.)

We ought to remember that these "documents" are the *supposed* ingredients of the Pentateuch. They do not exist separately but are the hypothetical results of scholarly analysis.

Sometimes, it appears, the material from one or the other of these documents is to be found in blocks of several stories. In the early chapters of Genesis, for example, we have a combination of J and P. The Creation story in Gen., ch. 1 (which goes to the first half of ch. 2:4) is P. We then have a long section of J, which begins with the words "In the day" in ch. 2:4 and goes through ch. 4:24. P takes up again at ch. 4:25 and goes through ch. 5. But the chapters listed below illustrate another fact. Sometimes two sources had the same story, and the two versions have been put together. The story of the

Flood is a good example. Beginning with Gen. 6:5 and going through ch. 9:17, this story is an interweaving of J and P. Both versions are complete, except that J does not tell of building the ark. If we separate them into two columns, the result is like this:

J	P
6:5-8	6:9-22
7:1-5	7:6
7:7	7:8-9
7:10	7:11
7:12	7:13-16a (to " command- ed him ")
7:16b-17	7:18
7:19	7:20-22
7:23	7:24 to 8:2a (to " were closed ")
8:2b (from " the rain ") -3a (to " continually ")	8:3b-5
8:6-12	8:13-19
8:20-22	9:1-17

If you will read each story separately, you will see their differences. The P story has one pair of each kind of animal and bird, a one-hundred-and-fifty-day flood which comes by the opening of " the windows of heaven " and the bursting forth of " the fountains of the great deep," and a great number of specific dates. The J story has seven pairs of clean and one pair of unclean animals, a forty-day flood caused by rain, and the familiar account of the birds going forth after the Flood. Seldom in the Pentateuch can two almost complete stories be found in what appears to the casual eye to be a single story. But it does happen now and then that two different versions of the same story have been dovetailed in such a way that we can separate the strands.

Some of the inconsistencies that were listed above are removed by this Documentary Hypothesis. The two covenants with Abraham are actually JE and P; the duplications of Jacob's change of name are E and P. The problem of Israel's population count in Egypt is resolved in noting that Ex. 1:15 is E and ch. 12:37 is P. And the difficulty occasioned by Ex. 6:2-3, where it is said that the patriarchs did not know Yahweh's name, is overcome when we realize that that passage is P — which never uses the name Yahweh in the book of Genesis. (It is fairly simple, even with the English translation, to determine sources in Genesis. Wherever you see " the LORD," you are reading J. Wherever you see " God," it is either E or P. If the narrative surrounding the use of " God " is quite detailed, with lists of everything that could be listed, with exact dates, and with a style that seems somewhat heavy and formalized, you are reading P.)

Nonetheless, problems remain in the documentary analysis of the Pentateuch. Some passages do not fit into any document. Such a one is Gen., ch. 14, which is the despair of many an Old Testament scholar; another is the narrative and oracles of Balaam in Num., chs. 22 to 24. Moreover, after Ex., ch. 3, where the E strand began to use the name Yahweh, it is very difficult to distinguish between E and J. The combination of E and J at the JE stage of development left only fragments and snatches of the E epic. And Deuteronomy, standing by itself, has left little if any trace in the first four books of the Pentateuch. But scholars generally feel quite confident that, with few exceptions, they can separate the strands into coherent and complete tales.

THE WAYS OF MEMORY

We have described the Documentary Hypothesis in some detail in order to make it clear that the problem of the writing of the Pentateuch is very complicated. We cannot assert that the Pentateuch is the work of a single author. As a matter of fact, we must go even beyond the " documents " to understand the significance of these books. Even if there were such epic writings as J, E, and P, they were not creations of men's imaginations but were the fruits of Israel's memory. Because this is the case, many students of the Old Testament interpret the growth of the Pentateuch without reference to the theory of J, E, D, and P. In the description that follows, this growth is interpreted according to " the ways of memory."

Basically, two different kinds of material appear in the Pentateuch: laws and narratives. The laws are clearly the product of centuries of development. They represent the " statute book " from several different kinds of societies in various periods in Israel's history. The familiar *Ten Commandments* (Ex. 20:1-17; Deut. 5:6-21) probably belong, in their original form (they have been expanded at several points), to the period when Israel was in the wilderness. Another group of laws, found in Ex. 20:23 to 23:19, is usually called the *Code of the Covenant*. The social order that the Code of the Covenant represents is clearly a settled, agricultural society. People own fields and vineyards (ch. 22:5), houses (v. 7), and slaves (ch. 21:2-11). There are three community festivals (ch. 23:14-17). Most scholars think that this code of laws represents the society of Israel during the period of the Judges and the early monarchy. The *book of Deuteronomy* is similar in many ways to the Code of the Covenant. But its laws, in chs. 12 to 26, represent a development on the Code of the Covenant. There is mention of the king (Deut. 17:14-20), and society is much more closely ordered. We can be fairly sure that Deuteronomy appeared during King Josiah's reform in 621 B.C. (II Kings, chs. 22 and 23), which explains why it is advanced over the earlier Code of the Covenant. Finally, there is the great body of *priestly law,* which occupies practically all of Leviticus and much of Exodus as well as part of Numbers. Although some of the priestly law is probably quite old, it did not receive its present form until after the exile in Babylon. In the legal material of the Pentateuch, therefore, we have evidence for many centuries of development.

Laws, in settled societies, tend to be written down as they are made. With narratives, however, it is quite different. We who are so used to the written word would find it all but impossible to get along without books. Israel seemingly did not find it impossible at all. Ancient men could not depend on written literature, because the vast majority could neither read nor write. They depended instead on the spoken word. The memory of Israel was passed on by word of mouth for centuries before it was written. It was oral tradition, that is, the memory of the past as stories spoken.

Once again, there are several kinds of stories in the oral traditions. Stories are remembered for different reasons. There seem, for example, to be what we may call *tribal hero-stories.* These are the tales of the great individuals of the past and their exploits. Modern examples would be the legends of Johnny Appleseed or Daniel Boone. Old Testament examples are the tales of Abraham, Isaac, and Jacob. Although these groups of narratives now have a religious meaning, they may have begun as hero-legends.

There are also *myths.* Myths are stories that reveal man's understanding of himself in relation to his world. They are tales that speak to him of his own experience, but that speak in universal terms. The stories of Creation, for example, are myths. They speak of man's awareness that he is one of God's creatures, and that he, of all the creatures, has a special responsibility in God's world. Sometimes myths also explain perplexing problems. Someone must have wondered why people speak different languages. The myth of the Tower of Babel (Gen. 11:1-9) answered the question.

Finally, there are what we may call *ritual legends*. These are the stories which were probably used in the religious festivals of Israel. At the festivals Israel remembered the great events of the past. In the time before the exile, there were three such festivals: Passover, which commemorated the exodus from Egypt; the Feast of Weeks, or Pentecost, which began as a harvest festival but seems to have become the remembrance of God's giving of the law on Mt. Sinai; and the Feast of Succoth, or Booths, which was originally the feast of the grape and grain harvests but became the commemoration of the wandering in the wilderness.

We should notice that the meanings of these feasts correspond to the three main subjects of the stories in Exodus and Numbers: the exodus (Ex., chs. 1 to 15), the establishment of the covenant on Mt. Sinai (Ex., chs. 16 to 20, with other stories scattered through the rest of Exodus and here and there in Leviticus), and the wandering in the wilderness (Num. 10:11 to the end of Numbers). Nothing would be more natural than that these festivals should see the reciting of the stories as part of the religious observance. Here, then, we may have the setting in which these tales took their shape.

It is probable also that the main sections developed inde pendently of each other. The ritual legends for the great religious festivals would have a certain connection, but the hero-legends and the myths originally had no relationship, even among themselves. Abraham's activities, for example, center at Hebron in central Judah, Isaac's at Beer-sheba in the territory of the tribe of Simeon, Jacob's around several places on the east side of the Jordan and around Shechem and Bethel in the territory occupied by the tribes of Ephraim and Manasseh. These tales therefore probably represent tribal traditions that were transmitted in the sanctuaries at which they center. The story of Joseph takes place in Egypt, but it possibly represents a hero-legend that was kept alive in the tribes of Ephraim and Manasseh, since Joseph, according to the tradition, was the father of Ephraim and Manasseh.

Such tales tend to grow. They usually begin with a nucleus of a good story, and as they are told and retold more details and incidents are added by the storytellers, until they emerge as whole tales, not biographies and not long enough to qualify as novels, but at least long short-stories. The Abraham stories provide a good example of this process. It seems likely that the core of the Abraham tradition is to be found in the story of the birth of Abraham's son. The story begins in Gen. 15:1-6, with God's promise of a son to the childless Abraham, and continues with the birth of Ishmael, who was the wrong son (ch. 16:1-15). Then God comes to Abraham near Hebron and promises him a son by Sarah. (Ch. 18:1-15.) This child is named Isaac. (Ch. 21:1-3, 6-7.) Sarah's insistence on the expulsion of Hagar and Ishmael (vs. 8-21) is balanced by God's command that Abraham sacrifice Isaac. At the last moment, Isaac is delivered from death. (Ch. 22:1-14.) This story, complete in itself, has a great many parallels with an old Canaanite legend of the birth of a son.

The Abraham tradition has received several very good stories, probably heard in Beer-sheba by storytellers from Hebron, that originally belonged to Isaac. (Chs. 20; 21:22-34.) Since Abraham is the greater figure, it is more likely that stories originally about the lesser man would be transferred to him than that his stories would be told of Isaac. The account of

Abraham's buying a cave at Hebron was a humorous addition. (Ch. 23:2-20.) The tale of battle with Eastern kings over Sodom and Gomorrah (ch. 14) provided the Abraham stories with a stirring military beginning. Abraham having now been linked with those two notorious centers of sin, the existing and well-known tradition of the destruction of Sodom and Gomorrah and of Lot's part in it was added (chs. 13:2, 5-13, 18; 18:16 to 19:38). By the time the story had grown this far, the exile was looming up, and the legendary figure of the Hebron sanctuary was made the bearer of a promise that Israel should possess the Land of Canaan (ch. 15:7-21). Probably in the exile Abraham was connected with Babylonia (Ur of the Chaldeans, chs. 11:27 to 12:5). All that remained was for the priestly writers after the exile to give him a prior claim on the old Jacob shrines at Shechem and Bethel (chs. 12:6-9; 13:3-4), to get him to Egypt and back (ch. 12:10-20), and to place the origin of circumcision in God's covenant with him (chs. 16:16 to 17:27).

The story was complete. From a simple hero-legend, it had developed into a tradition of God's covenantal promises. Was this dishonest manipulation of the facts? Not at all. The important thing was not the facts but the meaning.

THE FAITH OF MEMORY

It seems unlikely that the narratives of the Pentateuch were written down before the exile. The confidence in the spoken word, in the oral tradition, persisted until, as one scholar puts it, " there was a crisis of confidence, when faith in the spoken word began to waver, when there was fear that all might be forgotten." The supreme crisis of this kind came at the Babylonian exile, when the political existence of the Hebrew people was ended, when the cream of society was deported to a foreign land, and when war threatened the very existence of Israel. Here the tradition assumed great importance, for it was

FIRST UNITED PRESBYTERIAN CHURCH
2619 BROADWAY
OAKLAND 12, CALIFORNIA

the only evidence Israel had that God was really the master of her history. At this time many of the stories, told over and over for centuries, were written down. And they were seen in a new light. Abraham's desire for a son was answered by God's promise of descendants who would possess the Land of Canaan. The traditions of the exodus, the covenant, and the wandering in the wilderness were seen as the sources of hope that God would lead Israel out of her despair again to the Promised Land. And in the face of punishment, Israel listened again to the myths that told of sin, realizing more profoundly than ever that she was guilty.

The honor of the preservation of the tradition belongs to the priests. They probably wrote the stories down. And in the years after the exile, they were the ones who provided the only leadership that the people had. When Israel was nothing more than a province of the Persian Empire, no king could arise. The priests filled the breach, providing both the moral leadership and the spiritual daring of ordering the mass of Israel's tradition into one story. They emphasized the ancient understanding of the chosen people as it was set forth in the exodus traditions. They put the stories centering around God's choice of Abraham, Isaac, and Jacob into the order in which we now have them, providing connecting links of the father-son relationships and adding some traditions known to them. To preface the whole, they appended the ancient stories of the Creation and of the sin of man, adding lists of genealogies to tie up earliest man to the beginning of Israel's history in the patriarchs.

The book of Deuteronomy continues to stand by itself, a body of law that purports to be given by Moses immediately before the crossing of the Jordan into Canaan. But Deuteronomy had first belonged at the beginning of the history of Israel from the exodus to the exile (the books of Deuteronomy through II Kings). The priests, however, wanted to keep all the law together. Therefore, they severed Deuteronomy from its place in the history book, wrote an introduction to it which made it a " second law " (the literal meaning of " Deuteronomy ") given in Moab after the wilderness wandering, and appended the tradition of Moses' death (originally at the end of Numbers). The Pentateuch was now complete.

The Torah, then, represents first of all the voice of the faith of Israel. For it is the deposit of Israel's memory as it was recounted by numberless storytellers and remembered by the people themselves. And it is the voice of the priests, who listened to the tradition with devotion and sought to shape it so that it could regain the vitality with which it had spoken to Israel in time past.

Perhaps we can see in the three main sections of the Pentateuch the answers to three questions. To the question, Who is Israel? we have the answer of the exodus tradition: We are God's people, chosen by him in love and led through the wilderness. The prophets are full of this tradition, indicating that this question received its answer early in Israel's history. A second question arises in response to the first: If we are God's people, what is our place in mankind? This was the question asked principally in the exile, and to it the tradition answers: We are promised the land through God's ancient promise to Abraham. In this land, we shall bless the nations. Still a third question then arises: Why did God choose us for blessing? The response is: We know ourselves, like all men, to be guilty of willful departure from God's love and promise. Though he created us and all men, we have sought to rebel against him. This is the reason for Israel's existence. Through God's covenant with Israel, the sin of mankind will be overcome.

For the rest of this book, we shall be looking at these questions and their answers in the order stated here. It may seem strange to start with the exodus instead of with the Creation, but it seems that Israel knew the exodus and its meaning before they knew much of creation. We shall follow Israel through her memory.

CHAPTER 3   *Out of Egypt*

W<small>E START</small> with the book of Exodus because it seems that
the Hebrew people themselves began here. For when we ask,
Who is Israel? the answer invariably is, Israel is the people
whom God brought out of Egypt. The event of the exodus, together with the giving and receiving of the covenant, was always seen as the most significant event in Israel's history, the
event in which Israel came into existence.

MEETING GOD

Israel in Egypt! The phrase always brings to mind the en-
slaving tyrant. Israel had once been at peace, for Joseph had
been a high official in Egypt. Now, however, a new king arose
" who did not know Joseph " (Ex. 1:8). Exactly which Egyptian Pharaoh this was is a matter of some doubt; it was probably Seti I (1302–1290 B.C.). Archaeology shows that Seti un-
dertook to re-establish a northern capital at Tanis, which has
been identified with the city called Raamses in v. 11. Furthermore, the oppression of the Hebrews would be quite in line
with the character of Seti's reign.

The new king initiated a new situation. No longer were
the Israelites tolerated by the Egyptians. They were put to
work, and hard work it was. (V. 14.) Yet the Hebrews saw

fear on the part of the Egyptians. What could have been fearful about a very small Hebrew population, which could be adequately served by two midwives, is difficult to see. Yet do not tyrannies always operate on fear? At the rate at which the Hebrews were producing children, so the story goes, the Egyptians feared to be overrun, though there could actually have been little possibility of it. The Pharaoh ordered the slaughter of all boys under two years of age.

But one boy escaped, and that under the Pharaoh's nose. We cannot help sensing the wry humor with which it was told that Moses, who would lead Israel out of this slavery, was delivered from death by the daughter of the very man who had ordered his murder. The story is a charming one, and is somewhat similar to stories that are told of the humble beginnings of other ancient heroes. The best twist, of course, is that the daughter of the Pharaoh actually paid the baby's mother to nurse her own child. (Ch. 2:9.) But Moses, the first and perhaps the greatest of the Israelite leaders, retained forever an Egyptian name, Mose (Hebrew, *Mōsheh*), which we find in the names of kings such as Ahmose, Thutmose, and others.

Now we have the principal characters of the drama: Moses, the Pharaoh of Egypt, and the oppressed Hebrews. The conflict is heightened by Moses' murder of the sadistic Egyptian foreman (ch. 2:11-12) and by his forced flight from Egypt when the act had become known (vs. 13-15). With Moses' arrival in Midian, the stage is set for the next act.

As is usual, God enters the action in the course of men's daily, normal activities. Moses was out herding sheep near Mt. Horeb. The precise location of Mt. Horeb (or Sinai) is not certain. Exodus 3:1 puts it in the territory of Midian, which is across the Gulf of Aqabah from the Sinai peninsula. Wherever it may have been, what matters is what happened there.

The bush was the usual low, scraggly desert shrub; but this bush was different, burning with fire but not consumed. Our curiosity, like Moses', may be aroused by this thing, but like him we need to look beyond it. The burning bush was simply the means to attract Moses, and when he once confronted God, his amazement at the bush was replaced by amazement at the presence of God. Miracles in the Bible — if the bush is a miracle — are important only as they point beyond themselves to God's action.

First, Moses had to remember who he was. "Do not come near; put off your shoes from your feet, for the place on which you are standing is holy ground." (Ch. 3:5.) Men do not come casually to the holy. Mere curiosity is insufficient reason for approaching God. For God is God, and we are only men. Where God is, the awful holiness is, and we tread lightly. Indeed, like Moses, we hide our faces with fear. (V. 6.) Such fear is a combination of awe and deep reverence with true terror. Israel was never ashamed to admit that she feared God, for Israel was profoundly aware that man in the presence of God can make no claim to holiness.

Yet when we hear the message of the holy God, we hear the message of deliverance. "I have seen the affliction of my people who are in Egypt, . . . and I have come down to deliver them out of the hand of the Egyptians." (Vs. 7-8.) But there was more. Moses was given a command: "Come, I will send you to Pharaoh that you may bring forth my people, the sons of Israel, out of Egypt" (v. 10). God does not come to us to give us a "good feeling inside." He comes to set us to work, to doing what he wants done. The great experiences of religious life are real only if they issue in obedience.

But we hesitate to take up God's burden. "Who am I," Moses asked, "that I should go to Pharaoh, and bring the sons of Israel out of Egypt?" Moses knew his own inadequacies, but God knew the man he had chosen. And try as Moses might, he could not change God's mind. "How will I persuade them that I have been sent by God?" (v. 13) was the next question. Then, "But they won't listen to me" (ch. 4:1). Then, "But I'm not a good speaker" (v. 10). Finally, in desperation, "Oh, my Lord, send, I pray, some other person" (v. 13). God finds it necessary to beat down man's objections. When Moses complained that he was nobody, God answered, "But I will be with you" (ch. 3:12). If God is with us, who we are in ourselves matters not at all. When Moses wanted to know how to prove that he was really sent, God responded by telling him his name, Yahweh. In answer to the argument that the people would not listen, God gave him some magic with which to impress the people. To Moses' complaint of his inability to speak, God replied, much as he had to the first argument, "Now therefore go, and I will be with your mouth and teach you what you shall speak" (ch. 4:12). Finally, when Moses wished that God would find someone else for the job, God provided Moses' brother Aaron to do the talking. But Moses was not relieved of responsibility. He still had to go and carry the burden.

Here, then, the drama has begun. God has entered the picture, and the situation is changed. For the God whom Moses has met is Yahweh. This, at least, is probably how the word is to be pronounced. In later centuries, the name of God was thought by Jews too sacred to pronounce. When the word appeared in the text, they pronounced instead "Adonai," which means "Lord." (When in the Middle Ages the Hebrew script, which had been composed entirely of consonants, received vowel markings, the scribes put the vowels of Adonai with the consonants of Yahweh. In some English versions this has produced the word Jehovah, which is a monstrous hybrid, corresponding to nothing in heaven or on earth.)

Yahweh, it seems to have been. And it is related to that difficult expression of Ex. 3:14, "I AM WHO I AM," or "I WILL BE WHAT I WILL BE," or "I AM WHAT I AM." The name Yahweh is derived from the Hebrew verb "to be," and it means, "he causes to be." Since "to be" in Hebrew is "to act, to be active," "he causes to be" means "he makes things happen." As a matter of fact, with only a change of Hebrew vowels, the expression "I AM WHO I AM" would be read "I MAKE HAPPEN WHATEVER I MAKE HAPPEN." Yahweh is the God of history. To meet Yahweh is to meet the God who is known in the events that he brings to pass.

Is this a new God? No, say the storytellers. He is "the God of your fathers" (vs. 6, 15, 16). Moses is to come to the people, telling them that he has met their God and things are about to happen. When they want to know if he has really met their God, he will demonstrate it by pronouncing Yahweh's name. The very pronouncing of the name is to say, "He is about to cause something to happen." In the depth of despair, God sends the message of hope. To the miserable slaves God says, "I will deliver you."

But it is still no more than hope. As the drama moves on, it seems that men will do their best to frustrate God. Is God stronger than Egypt? To the Hebrew slaves it must have seemed doubtful. Is God stronger than any human tyranny? Sometimes we wonder. But then he brings us "out of Egypt."

OF HARDENED HEARTS

The first request for a "leave of absence" was summarily denied. Pharaoh first claimed ignorance of Yahweh. "Who is Yahweh, that I should heed his voice and let Israel go? I do not know Yahweh, and moreover I will not let Israel go." (Ch. 5:2.) When Moses and Aaron pressed the request, the Pharaoh argued that this was an excuse to get out of work.

" The people of the land are now many and you make them rest from their burdens!" (V. 5.) (A very slight alteration of one Hebrew word produces a better reading: "The people of the land are lazy as it is.")

The upshot of it was that the people had to do as much work as before, but they had to find their own straw for brick-making. When it took longer and the daily quota was not filled, the foremen received beatings for their pains. And when the foremen complained to the Pharaoh, they got the same answer: "You are idle, you are idle; therefore you say, 'Let us go and sacrifice to Yahweh'" (v. 17). Moses' own people turned upon him. His efforts to obtain their release had only angered the Pharaoh and made life even harder for the oppressed Israelites. "Yahweh look upon you and judge, because you have made us offensive in the sight of Pharaoh and his servants, and have put a sword in their hand to kill us." (V. 21.) Moses began to feel that his purpose might be frustrated as well by his own people as by the Egyptians.

The next act is the series of plagues that were brought upon Egypt. We need not concern ourselves too much with the details. The text of Ex., chs. 7 to 11, is dramatic enough. Many attempts have been made to connect the plagues with natural happenings in Egypt, but no such undertaking can be successful. The plagues represent the addition of detail to heighten the dramatic suspense of the hardening of Pharaoh's heart. His continued refusal to give in to the Israelites highlighted the power of Yahweh. Pharaoh was acting toward his slaves as if he were God. But his powerlessness before the real God only pointed up Yahweh's majesty: "By now I could have put forth my hand and struck you and your people with pestilence, and you would have been cut off from the earth; but for this purpose have I let you live, to show you my power, so that my name may be declared throughout all the earth.

You are still exalting yourself against my people, and will not let them go " (ch. 9:15-17). It is in the nature of men to cling to what they think belongs to them. It is in the nature of God to demand what is his. And the greatest nation is no match for God. The hardening of hearts can only delay God's plan; it cannot finally frustrate it.

PASSOVER

The last plague was the worst one. The first-born of every family in Egypt was to be killed, but those of the Israelites would be spared. At the sign of lamb's blood on the doorposts, Yahweh would " pass over " the house; whence the name later applied to the festival of remembrance: Passover.

And so it was. The appointed night came, the outburst of grief and mourning in Egypt rose in the night, and the terrified Egyptians urged the Israelites to go. Pharaoh himself, so the story goes, sent them out, with the curious, half-pathetic, and totally un-Egyptian remark, " And bless me also! " (ch. 12:32). They went east and south toward the Reed Sea (the English versions all have " Red Sea " in ch. 13:18, but the Hebrew is *yam sūph,* which is a sea or lake of reeds). The Reed Sea was probably one of a group of the lakes that used to be in the area where the Suez Canal now is. Shallow lakes they were, and not a serious barrier to travel. Later interpretation has made more of the " sea " than was actually there.

But the Pharaoh changed his mind once more, deciding to eliminate these troublesome Hebrews for good. He gathered his whole army for the campaign and could have massacred the Hebrews with no trouble. But for the last time Yahweh showed his " glory over Pharaoh " (ch. 14:4). The famous story of the crossing of the sea is familiar enough. There seem to be two versions of it in Ex., ch. 14. In one version, the parting of the waters was by " a strong east wind " (v. 21); in the other, by the magic of Moses' uplifted rod (v. 16). To be sure, the story has been expanded by devout imagination, but strong winds in the Suez area have been known to disperse the waters of these very shallow lakes. This, however, is far from the point of the story.

The point is that the escape from Egypt manifested Yahweh's gracious might. When the waters returned to the lake, the Egyptian troops were caught and drowned. The meaning of the story to Israel is clear. The Israelites escaped from Egypt not by their own strength but by Yahweh's. And they escaped, so they insisted, from an Egypt that was stubbornly against their going, but that could not resist Yahweh when he acted. Yahweh brought Israel out "by strength of hand" (ch. 13:14).

Here, then, is the starting point of Israel's experience. We cannot read the books of the Prophets or the book of The Psalms without stumbling over reference after reference to the exodus. Those who wrote and thought of the exodus saw it as *the* act of God that surpassed all other acts. The New Testament has such an event as well. The cross of Christ is the act of God that spells deliverance and salvation for Christians, just as the exodus spells deliverance and salvation for Jews. Indeed, the exodus and its meaning contributed much to the way in which the early church understood Jesus and described his life, death, and resurrection. The sacrament of the Lord's Supper derived from the Passover meal, which was the commemoration of the exodus. Both Paul and John speak of Jesus in terms of the "Passover lamb." (See John 1:29; 19:36 — a reference to the Passover lamb in Ex. 12:46; I Cor. 5:7, among other passages.) In the transfiguration story, where Moses and Elijah speak to Jesus "of his departure, which he was to accomplish at Jerusalem" (Luke 9:31), the Greek text reads literally, "of his exodus, which he was to fulfill at Jerusalem."

In these and in many other ways, the New Testament describes Christ as a "new exodus," which is the finest witness to the fact that the exodus was the great event in which Israel received salvation.

In the exodus God acted for his people, delivering them from slavery. But the mere event would have said nothing. Israel had to remember it. The way she remembered it was by the Feast of the Passover, which has always stood at the center of Jewish religion. Like most of the great festivals of the Hebrew people, Passover probably has a history that goes behind the exodus. It did not *begin* as the exodus memory; it *became* the exodus memory.

It seems clear that three separate ritual acts have been combined into Passover. One is the Dedication of the First-born (see Ex. 13:1-2, 11-16; 34:19-20; Deut. 15:19-23). Another is the Feast of Unleavened Bread (see Ex. 12:15-20; 13:3-10; 23:15; 34:18; Lev. 23:6-8; Deut. 16:3-4). The third is the Passover sacrifice (see Ex. 12:1-13, 21-27, 43-49; 34:25; Lev. 23:5; Num. 9:1-14; Deut. 16:1-2, 5-7).

The *Passover sacrifice* seems to have begun as the sacrifice of a lamb for the smearing of its blood on the lintels of the door. In primitive societies, this is often a means to keep evil spirits out of the house. The lamb may even have been slaughtered on the threshold of the house, since the word for "basin" in Ex. 12:22 may also mean "threshold." But in the remembrance of Israel's deliverance, the blood on the lintels became the sign of membership in God's people, the sign of a covenant. It is the distinguishing mark of those who belong to God. Again, this sacrifice probably began as a family ritual — as it is in Judaism today. Deuteronomy, however, prescribes its observance in the Temple. For a time at least, the Passover became a feast held in one place by the whole nation. The sacrifice was made in the Temple, and the blood was dashed against the altar instead of on doorposts. The meaning was the same. The act of sacrifice was the acceptance by men of God's purpose of salvation. " We belong to Yahweh," they proclaimed by their rite.

The *Feast of Unleavened Bread* was originally a feast of the barley harvest. But, like Israel's other feasts, it became the memory of an event in history. Its connection with Passover is that, as the story goes, " the people took their dough before it was leavened, their kneading bowls being bound up in their mantles on their shoulders " (Ex. 12:34). They had to be in a hurry, and there was no time to put leaven in the bread dough to make it rise, " because they were thrust out of Egypt and could not tarry, neither had they prepared for themselves any provisions " (v. 39). So the unleavened bread became a sign of their readiness to go whenever God commanded, without elaborate preparation for their comfort. " We belong to Yahweh," they proclaimed by their rite, " and we will go when and where he tells us, trusting him alone to provide for us."

The *Dedication of the First-born* may have its background in sacrifice. It is unpleasant to us to think that ancestors of the Hebrews may at one time have sacrificed their first children. The custom certainly ceased long before the people Israel came on the scene. But it is continued in the insistence that to Yahweh belong the first-born of animals and men. At one time, first-born sons may have been dedicated as priests, but later the tribe of Levi took over that position, and first-born sons were bought back from the priesthood by a payment (see Num. 3:40-51). In the context of the Passover, the dedication of the first-born to Yahweh is the response of gratitude that he had not killed Israel's first-born as he had those of the Egyptians (see Ex. 13:14-15). Israel herself cannot claim to be her own master. She is Yahweh's. " We belong to Yahweh," the people proclaimed by their rite. " We will go when and where he tells us, obeying him and offering ourselves to him in profound thanks."

The exodus tradition in Ex., chs. 1 to 15, is not merely the story of an astonishing deliverance from slavery. It is part and parcel of Israel's worship of God. The story has shaped the ritual. And the ritual has had a hand in shaping the story. But both say to us: "Yahweh is a God of deliverance. He delivers his people from bondage."

"I will sing to Yahweh, for he has triumphed gloriously;
   the horse and his rider he has thrown into the sea.
Yahweh is my strength and my song,
   and he has become my salvation;
this is my God, and I will praise him,
   my father's God, and I will exalt him. . . .
Who is like thee, O Yahweh, among the gods?
   Who is like thee, majestic in holiness,
      terrible in glorious deeds, doing wonders? . . .
Thou hast led in thy steadfast love the people whom thou
      hast redeemed,
   thou hast guided them by thy strength to thy holy
      abode. . . .
Yahweh will reign for ever and ever."

(Ex. 15:1-2, 11, 13, 18.)

So the people sang at the Passover Feast. They had come "out of Egypt."

CHAPTER 4 | *God's Own Possession*

W<small>E COME</small> now to the heart of the matter. God had only started with the deliverance of Israel from Egypt. More was to be done. The great deed had to be sealed in Israel's heart and mind, just as the redemption wrought by Christ on the cross must be sealed to us by our acceptance of the vows of faith and obedience. The completion of the event of deliverance is to be found in the establishment of the covenant.

Covenant is a word that is difficult to define. In some ancient texts, a covenant seems to be a bargain or a contract, a business affair in which one party promises to deliver goods or services and the other promises to pay for them. Sometimes the Old Testament approaches this idea, when it seems that God must reward Israel with prosperity if Israel obeys his commandments. The covenant is often, however, much closer to a treaty between nations. Sometimes two nations of equal power join in a "mutual assistance pact," in which each promises aid to the other if he needs it. But recent study of ancient treaty forms has shown another kind that comes closer to the Old Testament covenant idea. In this kind of treaty, a great nation offers protection to a small one in return for fidelity and (usually) taxes. By the same token, God comes to Israel with the offer of his divine presence, to which Israel must in turn give her obedience and loyalty. The covenant begins with God's act and continues with Israel's response.

The Initiative of God

Yahweh is "he who makes things happen." This is the center of Israel's understanding of God. As we can see from the stories of Israel's murmuring in the wilderness (Ex. 16:1 to 17:7), if Israel were to have her own way, nothing at all would happen. Israel would return to Egypt. And we shall see later that Israel "griped" in this way many times.

But the fact is that God has acted, and this realization forms the foundation stone of Israel's faith. For this faith is based on what is actual. Israel was not engaged in a search for God. God had done the searching, and God had found Israel. The covenant came about because of grace.

> "You have seen what I did to the Egyptians, and how I bore you on eagles' wings and brought you to myself. Now therefore, if you will obey my voice and keep my covenant, you shall be my own possession among all peoples; for all the earth is mine, and you shall be to me a kingdom of priests and a holy nation." (Ex. 19:4-6.)

God was acting toward Israel not merely to display power or to awe her. He carried Israel as an eagle carries his young.

> "Like an eagle that stirs up its nest,
>   that flutters over its young,
> spreading out its wings, catching them,
>   bearing them on its pinions,
> Yahweh alone did lead him,
>   and there was no foreign god with him."
>
> (Deut. 32:11-12.)

This was not a relationship that Israel sought. The covenant is primarily the act of God by which he takes a people to be his "own possession among all peoples." The King James Version translates "my own possession" as "a peculiar treasure unto me." Israel is a possession dear to her owner, not so much because of intrinsic value as because of his attachment to her. Yahweh chose Israel rather than another nation. Why did he choose Israel? The question cannot really be answered.

> "You are a people holy to Yahweh your God;
> Yahweh your God has chosen you to be a people
> for his own possession, out of all the peoples that
> are on the face of the earth. It was not because
> you were more in number than any other people
> that Yahweh set his love upon you and chose you,
> for you were the fewest of all peoples; but it is
> because Yahweh loves you." (Deut. 7:6-8.)

Israel cannot claim consideration for her size. Nor can she claim consideration for her goodness.

> "Know therefore, that Yahweh your God is not
> giving you this good land to possess because of
> your righteousness; for you are a stubborn people."
> (Deut. 9:6.)

We may recall Paul's words:

> "God chose what is foolish in the world to shame
> the wise, God chose what is weak in the world to
> shame the strong, God chose what is low and de-
> spised in the world, even things that are not, to
> bring to nothing things that are, so that no human
> being might boast in the presence of God" (I Cor.
> 1:27-29).

No human reason can account for God's choice of Israel. We sometimes hear it said that God has had many chosen peoples in this world: the Greeks were chosen because of their genius for beauty and philosophy; the Romans, because of their genius for law and order; the Hebrews, for their genius for religion. But the Hebrews had no genius for religion. Their religion is no more impressive than any other religion. They brought to it nothing more than men everywhere bring to their religion. Yet God chose them, not because they already had something important to offer but because he loved them and because he had the supremely important gift to offer, the relationship of love with himself. This is what Christians mean by grace. It is God, taking the initiative and coming to his people so that he may give them what they cannot earn for themselves. If, after all, we cannot earn the love of our fellow men, how can we earn God's love? But we need not wait until we can earn it. God has already offered it. He came to make a motley conglomeration of wanderers on the earth into "a holy nation." Note that this is a *nation,* a community of people bound into a real unit, not simply a group of individuals. So Christ founded his church not as the sum of many individual believers but as a community where many have become "one body." And this nation is a *holy* nation, a nation that, if we may believe scholarly explanations of the word "holy," is a nation "separated out" from the others for a specific task. Israel is chosen not so that she may pat herself on the back but so that she may fulfill a responsibility. Grace checks and humbles our pride. It issues in an answer, in a response.

The Heart of a Nation

From the beginning, we may believe, Israel understood the content of the covenant to be law. We Christians often vastly misunderstand the whole idea of law. We think that law means legalism, that obedience to the law means necessarily the anxiety about externals. Christ has delivered us from legalism, but we cannot escape from *law* in its true sense. Israel did not concoct her law in order that she might achieve God's love. She developed it in response to a love that she had already received. It was by means of the law that Israel lived out the life of faith. To be sure, legalism sometimes entered in, particularly when the assertion was made that: "If you will obey my commandments which I command you this day, to love Yahweh your God, and to serve him with all your heart and with all your soul, he will give the rain for your land in its season. . . . And he will give grass in your fields for your cattle, and you shall eat and be full" (Deut. 11:13-15). There obedience becomes the means to prosperity. When we are faithful in order to receive our reward, then we are legalists. But when we seek a true and proper discipline for our life of response to God's grace, law provides us with guides to joyful responsibility.

Law and Worship. The Hebrews were very careful to avoid a difference between "Sunday piety" and "weekday living." The law of the Old Testament is set squarely in the context of worship. This is clear from three facts:

1. *The law is always given after an appearance of God and as his word to Israel.* The Ten Commandments are placed after Yahweh's first descent to the top of Mt. Sinai (Ex. 19:16-25). The Code of the Covenant follows "the thunderings and the lightnings" on the mountain (ch. 20:18-21). The major body of the priestly law follows first upon a meal in God's presence (ch. 24:1-11), then upon God's appearing in glory to Moses (chs. 33:1 to 34:9). The law of Deuteronomy is preceded by the narrative of God's majestic appearance on Mt. Horeb (Deut. 4:9-24; 5:1-5).

2. *The law is the ingredient of a ceremony of remembrance*

and renewal. We know that in later times the Feast of Pentecost was the remembrance of the giving of the law. A number of references elsewhere in the Old Testament suggest very strongly that early in Israel's history there was a festival of covenant renewal (see, for example, Josh., ch. 24). We may believe that the reading of the narratives at such a ceremony included the reading of laws. That this happened on several occasions we know. Josiah read the law of Deuteronomy to the people in a great and pivotal covenant renewal ceremony (II Kings 23:1-3), and Ezra read what was probably the priestly law after the exile (Neh. 8:1-8).

3. *All the law codes affirm that faithfulness to God is Israel's first duty.* The Ten Commandments begin with four laws regarding Israel's relationship to God. The Code of the Covenant begins and ends with laws regarding worship. The priestly laws have much to say about the Tabernacle and the laws of sacrifice, of cleanliness, of atonement. The law code of Deuteronomy (chs. 12 to 26, though there is law in the earlier chapters as well) begins with the demand for pure and undefiled worship. Man's responsibility to man is the "second" commandment, as Jesus put it. It is not therefore less important than the first. But man's ethical life in relation to his fellow men must proceed from his religious life in relation to God.

Responsibility to God. The law is the response to Yahweh's covenant of grace. "I am Yahweh your God, who brought you out of the land of Egypt, out of the house of bondage." (Ex. 20:2.) Israel obeys the law in reference to the historic deed of God. Yahweh is her God. "You shall have no other gods before me." (Ex. 20:3.) This is not a philosophical statement of monotheism. It says, literally, "There shall be to you no other gods in my presence." That is, so far as Israel is concerned there are no other gods. No others may be worshiped, for where Yahweh is, no room remains for any other objects of worship. Yahweh demands the whole heart and soul and might. (Deut. 6:4.) Israel must root out all traces of the worship of other gods in her midst. (Ch. 12.) We can illustrate this by human marriage (as did the prophet Hosea). When one falls in love, he does not do so halfheartedly. He does not say to his wife, " My dear, I love you with part of myself, but the rest I will keep back in case I should fall in love with some other woman." He gives himself, and she gives herself, each wholeheartedly and with such devotion that neither could possibly love any other. So it is with devotion to God. Israel belongs to him and to no other; *for her* there is no god but Yahweh.

To be sure, Israel often failed. While she was still at the holy mountain, the temptation became too great. When Moses lingered at the top, the people became discouraged with Yahweh and demanded the kind of god they could see. Aaron supplied them with such a god in the golden calf. (Ex., ch. 32.) Yahweh could not let this faithlessness go unpunished. But though he punished the Israelites for their idolatry, he did not break the covenant. The demand still stood: " You shall not make yourself a graven image " (ch. 20:4). We cannot picture God, for God will not be confined to the limits of our imagination. Of course, an image had its magic implications. If you could make the god with your hands, you could control him. And Yahweh cannot be controlled by men. In the covenant relationship, Israel let herself be controlled by Yahweh.

Worship, then, was important to Israel because in it she remembered God's works and words and participated again in the ancient deeds of God's grace. Much of the law has to do with worship. And although we may become impatient over the myriad details of the worship laws, we must understand that these details were included to ensure that Israel would not worship God casually or wrongly. One does not " take the name of Yahweh . . . in vain " (Ex. 20:7). He does not swear a casual oath by Yahweh; nor does he use the name of God for what is unworthy of God. The Sabbath too is kept " holy." It is a day different from the others, in that man rests from his work (this is the literal meaning of Sabbath). And on that day, in remembrance of the holy God's work in Israel's history (Deut. 5:12-15), he pays God honor. This is the intention of all worship. When a man brings an animal for sacrifice (Lev., ch. 1), he brings Yahweh not any one chosen at random but the best of the flock, the one without blemish. To give God the property that you would sell at a discount would be to count God less worthy than your customer. We need not linger over the details of worship. The laws are not very interesting reading, save for the specialist, and they contain many prescriptions whose reason escapes us. No one should feel guilty if he cannot make much out of Leviticus.

There are two elements of Israel's early worship, though, that ought to detain us for a moment. They are the Ark and the Tent of Meeting. The Ark (sometimes called the Ark of the Covenant) has been thought by most recent scholars to have been a box which the Hebrews viewed as the throne of the invisible God. According to Deuteronomy and the priestly tradition, the Tables of the Law were kept in it. (Ex. 40:20; Deut. 10:1-5.) The Ark had much to do with warfare, and it was thought to be the focus of God's presence in battle (Num. 10:35-36), as several tales from Israel's later history show. It remained the symbol of God's presence and of the expression of his will in law, and it was thus a center for worship.

The Tent of Meeting may originally have been a different object altogether. Those who desired to " consult Yahweh " (Ex. 33:7-11) went to it. There oracles from God, the omens of the future and the demands of the present, were received.

As such the Tent of Meeting occupied an important place in Israel's worship. In the latest period, the priestly editors combined the Ark and the Tent into a very elaborate Tabernacle, the detailed specifications of which are in Ex., chs. 25 to 31 and chs. 35 to 40.

These objects stood in Israel's midst as reminders of her responsibility to God. Worship and faithfulness were her watchwords.

Responsibility to Man. The covenant does not stop with our responsibilities of worship. Rather, it proceeds, as it must, into all of life. To be responsible to God is to be responsible to men. There is no gap between the people at worship and the people in daily life. All of life comes under the covenant.

The last six commandments of the Decalogue deal with the integrity of society. They begin with the family (Ex. 20:12), which was always the most important human relationship. Indeed, there is an interesting difference here between Hebrew law and other ancient law. In the Hammurabi Code, a code of law from Babylonia about 1700 B.C., crimes punishable by death are: incest, connivance in the murder of one's husband, house construction whose faults cause the death of the owner, and theft. In the Code of the Covenant, crimes punishable by death are: murder, striking or cursing the parents, slave-stealing, sorcery, idolatry, sexual relations with animals, and possession of a free, goring ox after warning. Three of these proscriptions have to do with perverted worship, and the others deal with human relations. The Babylonians thought that a man's property was the more important; the Hebrews valued the man more highly. This is also clear in the Ten Commandments. To be sure, " you shall not steal " (Ex. 20:15), but the other commandments concern human relationships: the parents (v. 12), the life of man (v. 13), the marriage relation (v. 14), matters affecting justice (v. 16), and the coveting of another's goods or relations (v. 17). Human relationships extend even to one's inner thoughts. The unspoken or unacted attitude is as important as the overt crime. To covet what is someone else's shatters the integrity of society as much as to steal.

In the law of Deuteronomy, the problem of human relations is attacked from a slightly different angle. Whereas in the Ten Commandments and in the Code of the Covenant society was to maintain its integrity as a pure means of response to Yahweh, the Deuteronomic law connects human responsibility with Israel's memory. The harvester of grain, olives, or grapes is to leave some produce for " the sojourner, the fatherless, and the widow," because "you shall remember that you were a slave in Egypt and Yahweh your God redeemed you " (Deut. 24:19-22). Israel has known what it is to be a slave, to be poor, to be alien, to be downtrodden. And because Yahweh delivered Israel, Israel is to return justice to those whom society might view as worthless. " Justice, and only justice, you shall follow, that you may live and inherit the land which Yahweh your God gives you." (Ch. 16:20.) The humanitarianism of Deuteronomy is one of its most striking characteristics. The Code of the Covenant had prescribed that a Hebrew slave should be set free after six years (Ex. 21:2), but Deuteronomy adds that he is to be furnished " liberally out of your flock, out of your threshing floor, and out of your wine press " (Deut. 15:14). But Deuteronomy is no less severe than before on the defilement of Israel. Nothing is to be entertained that would make the good land that Yahweh has given his people unclean. " For you are a people holy to Yahweh." (Chs. 7:6; 14:2.)

Still another approach to human responsibility is to be found in the priestly law. The priests did not include very much new law in this respect, but one very important group of laws is Lev., ch. 19, which is part of a special code known as the Holiness Code (chs. 17 to 26). The reason for moral society in this document is holiness. "You shall be holy; for I Yahweh your God am holy." (Ch. 19:2.) If Israel is the people of a holy God, she must exhibit holiness in everything she does, in her care for the poor (vs. 9-10), in her truthfulness (vs. 11-12), in her economic and charitable life (vs. 15-16), and in the attitudes of her mind toward others (vs. 17-18). "You shall love your neighbor as yourself." Why? Because "I am Yahweh." Only Yahweh is God, and man's relation to his fellows must reflect their common submission to God and their common responsibility to one another as equals before God.

The thrust of Hebrew law is to provide a framework in which responsible life may be lived. If Israel is the covenant people, she must act the part. We do not accept grace and sit back. God's action for us impels us forward to action in response. Let us never look patronizingly at the diligence of the Jew, who formulated regulations and took care to abide by them in order that he might serve God. If the law says nothing else it says this to us: "Your life belongs to another. You may not order your life apart from the demand of God and the need of others." Let our diligence in obedience be the equal of theirs who developed and obeyed the law.

MURMURING AND MERCY

We do not know very much about the wandering between Mt. Sinai and the Land of Canaan. The impression that several of the prophets give, that this was the time when Israel was closest to Yahweh (see Hos. 2:15; Amos 5:25; Jer. 2:2), is belied by the narratives in Numbers. There the wandering is told as a series of complaints, defeats, and punishments for unfaithfulness. It is quite a discouraging account.

The emotion of a religious experience is the hardest emotion to keep alive. And the difficulty increases under conditions of adversity. No sooner had Israel begun the journey to Canaan than the people complained at misfortune. Numbers 11:1-3 tells of the first such complaint, when Yahweh sent fire and the place was called Taberah, or Burning (see also Deut. 9:22). Immediately afterward the people complained of the food (is not that typical?). "We remember the fish we ate in Egypt for nothing, the cucumbers, the melons, the leeks, the onions, and the garlic; but now our strength is dried up, and there is nothing at all but this manna to look at." (Num. 11:5-6.) Yahweh provided quail in such numbers that the people gorged themselves and became sick (vs. 31-33). Miriam and Aaron were the next to complain, feeling that Moses was receiving some credit that they should have (ch. 12:1-2).

By this time Israel seems to have reached the oasis of Kadesh, where she apparently spent some years. Some scholars feel that of the traditional forty years in the wilderness, at least thirty-eight were passed at Kadesh. But this is to take the forty years too literally. "Forty" in the Bible is a round number, and forty years is nothing but a "long time," about the span of one generation. Kadesh was somewhere in the wilderness south of Beer-sheba, though no one is absolutely certain where; an oasis that the Arabs call 'Ain Kadis has been suggested as the place. Here it was that Moses sought to consolidate the motley tribes of the exodus. It was a consolidation wrought through more dissension and suffering.

From Kadesh the spies were sent north to scout the Land of Canaan (ch. 13:1-24). The report they brought back was both encouraging and discouraging. The land, they said, "flows with milk and honey, and this [a huge cluster of grapes] is its fruit" (v. 27). Some of the spies told tall tales of giants who inhabited the place (v. 32), and some were confident of success (v. 30). The people believed the pessimists, and they were all for deposing Moses and returning to Egypt (ch. 14:2-4). When, however, Yahweh promised that none of those then alive except Joshua and Caleb (the optimistic spies) would see Canaan, they reversed themselves completely. "See, we are here, we will go up to the place which Yahweh has promised." (V. 40.) But halfhearted repentance produces halfhearted invasion, and they were soundly beaten (v. 45).

At Kadesh also was the rebellion of Korah, Dathan, and Abiram. (Ch. 16.) Two separate rebellions are probably combined here. Korah's rebellion was over Moses' and Aaron's priesthood. (V. 3.) Since Moses refused the duties of priesthood to the Levites (vs. 9-10), the story clearly belongs to the priestly strand. The rebellion of Dathan and Abiram, on the other hand, was a political revolt. Moses, they claimed, had not made good on his "campaign promises" (vs. 13-14).

The last murmuring at Kadesh concerned the lack of water. (Ch. 20:2-13.) Here Moses produced water from the rock, as he had at Massah. (Ex. 17:1-7.) There, as here, the place is also called Meribah ("contention"). Possibly the two accounts of Moses' bringing forth water from rock go back to one such story. Moses, however, was punished for his arrogance in taking credit for the miracle (Num. 20:10), and he was not permitted to enter the Promised Land (v. 12).

From these traditions of the sojourn in Kadesh, we may catch a glimpse of a very difficult time of organization. People look after their own interests, and individual interest frequently sets a roadblock before God's purpose. We may wonder that God did not throw up his hands and give Israel over to final destruction. Destruction there was, in plenty. Each murmuring was answered by punishment. But God's punishment is never the end of his dealings with men. The wandering traditions are full of mercy.

Moses sometimes had to persuade God to be faithful to his

covenant promises. (Num. 14:13-19.) Perhaps this is offensive to us. Do the prayers of men change God's mind? We often hear that "prayer changes things." If this were so, prayer would be nothing but magic. Yet we believe that God answers prayer. In this case, God changed his mind. Was it because of Moses' prayer? Or was it because of God's "steadfast love" (v. 19)? "Ask," said Jesus, "and it will be given you."

But God gave even when the people complained. He sent quail for them to eat, even though it made them ill. He continued to provide manna for them. When the plague of the "fiery serpents" (perhaps a fever of some sort) came among them, God told Moses to make the bronze serpent which saved those with the fever who looked upon it. (Ch. 21:6-9.) This example of sympathetic magic is a strange tale and perhaps quite ancient.

And God continued with his people. Though they would sometimes prefer to throw over the covenant and go back to Egypt, he was faithful to his promise to lead Israel into her Promised Land. Though the generation that saw the exodus was barred from entering Canaan, their children would be able to, and the promise would not be broken. And as Israel came closer to Canaan, success increased. Perhaps the internal dissension had been overcome. Perhaps the knowledge that the land lay just over a few hills and across the Jordan spurred them to greater efforts. They were able to bypass Edom, to go unmolested through Moab, to overcome Sihon, king of the Amorites, and Og, king of Bashan (whose claim to fame was the great size of his bed, Deut. 3:11).

Nothing, it seems, could now deter God's people from the conquest of their land. This is the theme of the stories of Balaam. (Num., chs. 22 to 24.) The age of these stories and oracles is much disputed. Some scholars put them at the time of the wilderness wandering itself, in the 1200's B.C. Others think that the stories may be very old but the oracles very late. References in the oracles to Israel's king (chs. 23:21; 24:7, 17) and to Assyria (ch. 24:22) indicate that at least the oracles must be dated much later, perhaps even after the exile.

The point, however, is clear enough. Balak, the Moabite prince, sent to Mesopotamia for Balaam, the famous diviner. Balaam, whose journey was hindered by God, finally arrived to do his prophesying and to collect his fee. Balaam had been hired to curse Israel, but Yahweh had commanded him to bless.

" How can I curse whom God has not cursed?
　　How can I denounce whom Yahweh has not denounced?"
　　　　　　　　　　　　　　　　　　　　　(Ch. 23:8.)

Balaam's refusal to curse Israel made Balak very angry; we can fairly see him jumping up and down in frustrated rage. But Balaam was unmoved.

　　　　" Behold, I received a command to bless;
　　　　　　he has blessed, and I cannot revoke it."
　　　　　　　　　　　　　　　　　(Ch. 23:20.)

　　　　" Blessed be every one who blesses you,
　　　　　　and cursed be every one who curses you."
　　　　　　　　　　　　　　　　　(Ch. 24:9.)

Balak's effort to provide the curse that would wither Israel away had been unavailing. He had paid Balaam well, and had sacrificed animal after animal to achieve the curse on Israel. But it does man no good to weary himself opposing God's intentions. Israel had been set on her path by God himself. And neither Moab nor Israel herself nor any other nation could finally hinder God's purpose. To the Promised Land the tribes went.

CHAPTER 5 | *Promise and Blessing*

God chose Israel to be his own people, the nation of his purpose. A nation, of course, needs territory if it is to be like other nations. And we left Israel in the last chapter on the verge of crossing the Jordan River into the Land of Canaan. Lest anyone be in suspense, The Book of Joshua goes on to tell of the successful conquest.

A question, nonetheless, needs answering: By what right does Israel possess Canaan? This question became of very great importance at the time of the exile, for Israel's possession of her land hung in the balance. Her right of conquest could hold good only as long as another nation did not come and conquer her. In the early years of the sixth century B.C., the Babylonians were conquering, and Israel's claim to Canaan seemed no stronger than anyone else's. Was there not a better reason for Israel's possession of the land? It was at this time that the traditions of God's choosing the patriarchs, Abraham, Isaac, and Jacob, became important. After Jerusalem had fallen in 586 B.C., Ezekiel said: "The word of the Lord came to me: 'Son of man, the inhabitants of these waste places in the land of Israel keep saying, "Abraham was only one man, yet he got possession of the land; but we are many; the land is surely given us to possess"'" (Ezek. 33:23, 24).

THE PROMISED LAND

The history of America is a story of men moving out into the wilderness and conquering it. The pioneers made a land out of forests, prairies, mountains, and deserts. Now that there is no land left for pioneers to move to, we find a certain nostalgia in watching " Westerns " on television or reading them in inexpensive books.

The history of the ancient world is quite the opposite. It is the story of men moving out of the wilderness into the realms of civilization. Someone has called ancient Near Eastern history the struggle between " the Desert and the Sown," between the nomads who sought security and the farmers who sought to keep what security they had. This is the pattern which we see in Israel's history. The Promised Land was not a new land awaiting development but an old land offering ready-made comfort.

But the Hebrews, unlike most ancient peoples, never forgot their desert background. " A wandering Aramean was my father," goes the beginning of an ancient festival recitation (Deut. 26:5), and it ends, " And he brought us into this place and gave us this land, a land flowing with milk and honey " (v. 9). The " wandering Aramean " is Jacob, and the picture we get of Abraham, Isaac, and Jacob is precisely the picture of nomads, constantly on the move, living in tents, and making their livelihood by herding sheep and goats. Though Abraham spends most of his time at Hebron, he moves from southern Mesopotamia to Haran in northern Mesopotamia, then to central Palestine and to Egypt. Returning, he divides his time between Hebron and the area around Beer-sheba. Isaac lives very close to Beer-sheba for his whole life, but Jacob wanders to Syria, back to the territory east of the Jordan, and into and around central Palestine. Only Lot settles for city life, but his

sojourn is interrupted. (Gen., ch. 19.) Israel began, so these
stories show, in the nomadic life of travel and tents, of dan-
ger and uncertainty. Indeed, the stories of the patriarchs may
reflect not the lives of individual men but the movements of
tribes and clans.

The nomad always looks on civilization as a dream on the
horizon, a vision of certainty and safety that he covets for himself. It is not strange, then, that ancient Near Eastern history
should be dotted with invasions of nomads from the desert
into agrarian lands. The conquest of Canaan by the Israelite
tribes is a case in point. We sometimes get the idea, influ-
enced by our knowledge of American frontier days, that Israel
was moving into a land all but uninhabited. On the contrary,
Canaan was inhabited by peoples who had been there over
long centuries, who had erected a culture that was highly so-
phisticated, although not the equal of the massive cultures of
Sumer, Babylonia, Egypt, and the Hittites. The Hebrews, in
taking this land, fell heir to its culture, and one of the major
tensions after the conquest lay in the contradiction between
Yahweh, the stern desert God of history, and Baal, the Canaanite god of fertility.

It was the God of history who moved the patriarchs. A nation was to be born. This nation would fulfill its role in the
Land of Canaan. This is the first part of God's promise to
Abraham. "Go from your country and your kindred and
your father's house to the land that I will show you." (Gen.
12:1.) "Lift up your eyes, and look from the place where you
are, northward and southward and eastward and westward;
for all the land which you see I will give to you and to your
descendants for ever." (Ch. 13:14-15.) The boundaries are
more clearly set out when Yahweh makes the covenant with
Abraham: "from the river of Egypt [probably the Wâdī el-
'Arîsh, south of Gaza, which is properly the "Brook of

Egypt"] to the great river, the river Euphrates" (ch. 15:18). At one time David's realm extended north very close to the Euphrates. The promise, then, looks forward to the day when Israel will not only possess her own land but will possess it in its broadest extent.

But for Abraham it is only a promise. The land is not his. He must even haggle with Ephron the Hittite for a cave in which to bury his wife. (Gen., ch. 23.) And Isaac must move from one well to another because the inhabitants of the land continually claim the wells that he has dug as their own. (Ch. 26:17-22.) Jacob, too, feeling that he is settled at Shechem, is beset by contention with the inhabitants (Gen., ch. 34) and must move on to Bethel. But even from Bethel he wanders on. (Ch. 35:16-21.) The promise of the land is only a promise. And though Israel settled comfortably into the routines of civilization, she could never forget her nomadic ancestry. History intervened to keep Israel from becoming too complacent in her possession of the Land of Canaan. The Promised Land was always over the next hill.

Sons and Heirs

A promised land, however, must have inhabitants. The difficulty for Abraham, as we have seen before (Chapter 2), was that he had no heir. "I will make of you a great nation" is the second part of God's promise. (Gen. 12:2, and see ch. 13:16.) This was all very well. But Abraham had yet to see it. "O Lord God, what wilt thou give me, for I continue childless . . . ? Behold, thou hast given me no offspring; and a slave born in my house will be my heir." (Ch. 15:2-3.) "Look toward heaven," Yahweh told him, "and number the stars, if you are able to number them. . . . So shall your descendants be." (Ch. 15:5.) And Abraham "believed" God. Not that Abraham merely believed that what Yahweh had said was true; he " had faith " in Yahweh. Only Yahweh himself could make good on his promises. In the other covenant passage, God changed Abraham's name on the strength of the promise: " No longer shall your name be Abram [perhaps " exalted father "], but your name shall be Abraham; for I have made you the father of a multitude of nations " (ch. 17:5). The name " Abraham " does not mean " father of a multitude " (Hebrew, *'āb-hāmôn*), but no one has yet been able to explain what it does mean.

Ishmael had been born, of course. But this was not enough, for Ishmael was the son of the slave Hagar. When, however, the son of Sarah was born, through Yahweh's intervention, he was named Isaac (" he laughs "), because his promised birth was greeted with laughter by Sarah (ch. 18:12) and by Abraham (ch. 17:17). Already we can see the process of selection going on. Abraham had been the one son of Terah who was chosen. (Ch. 11:27-32.) Now Isaac, not Ishmael, followed in the promise to Abraham. (Ch. 21:12.) Ishmael too became a great nation (ch. 21:18), but his descendants were not among the covenant people. Their names indicate that Ishmael was taken to be the father of the Arabs. (Ch. 25:12-16.)

With Isaac's sons, the process of selection continued. Twins were born to Rebekah. The elder was Esau; the younger, Jacob. According to custom, the eldest son is the heir. But Jacob followed his mother's unscrupulous advice. He first bought Esau's right of inheritance with a bowl of lentil soup. (Ch. 25:29-34.) Then, by trickery, he received the blessing of Isaac, the blessing that was supposed to assure good fortune and that was reserved for the elder son. (Ch. 27:1-40.) His forced flight to Aram was well timed. But we see again that a selection had been made. The normal pattern of inheritance was broken, and Jacob became the heir of the covenant with Abraham. Esau, the tricked brother, remained angry, and it was not by chance that Israel's tradition identified Esau as the father of the Edomites (ch. 36); for the Edomites were at enmity with Israel for centuries. (Even in New Testament times, one of the complaints the Jewish people made about King Herod was that his family was Idumaean, that is, of Edom.) But Jacob became "Israel." (Chs. 32:28; 35:10.) The selection was complete. And the twelve sons of Jacob-Israel made up the nation as the nation saw itself.

The birth of Jacob's sons, as tradition gives it to us, is also a tale of frustration and no little woe. Jacob's first love was Rachel, and he served Laban, his prospective father-in-law, seven years in order to pay the marriage price. (Ch. 29:15-20.) But when the wedding came, Laban slipped his older daughter, Leah, instead of Rachel, into Jacob's tent. On Jacob's furious accusation, Laban blandly assured him that one could not flout custom by giving a younger daughter in marriage before an older one. (Leah's chances of marriage may have been slight, since she was probably quite nearsighted [ch. 29:17].) Seven more years of free work, and Jacob received the wife he wanted. But Rachel had no children. Leah, on the other hand, provided Jacob with four sons. Since a wife's usefulness to the family and to society was measured in those days by her bearing of sons, Leah, unloved though she was, was proving very helpful. Four more sons were born to the maids of Leah and Rachel (ch. 30:1-13), two more sons and a daughter to Leah (ch. 30:17-21), and finally Rachel bore a son, Joseph (ch. 30:22-24). Last of all, after many travels and trials, Rachel died bearing Benjamin (ch. 35:16-18).

The number twelve seems to have been important to the Hebrews. The nation of Israel always maintained twelve tribes. With the birth of Joseph, Jacob had twelve children — eleven sons and a daughter, Dinah. But at Shechem there was trouble over Dinah. (Gen., ch. 34.) Perhaps Dinah was a tribe that ceased to exist, and Benjamin, " born " later, came in to take the vacant place. It is probable that the fortunes of the sons of Jacob reflect tribal rather than individual history. When the tribe of Levi assumed the priesthood for the entire nation and therefore forfeited its claim to territory (see Num. 3:11-13), only eleven tribes were left. The tribes of Ephraim and Manasseh then became full tribes in their own right, since it was they who made up the tribe of Joseph. (Whereas the list of tribes in Gen. 35:22-26 contains the names of both Joseph and Levi, that in Num., ch. 1, contains Ephraim and Manasseh, but neither Joseph nor Levi.)

All of this is simply to say that Israel traced her lineage back to the fathers to whom the promise had been given. The covenant of Yahweh with Abraham promised that Abraham would be " a great nation." Now, Israel said, we are the living proof that Yahweh keeps his promises.

The Agent of Blessing

The third part of Yahweh's promise to Abraham is filled with blessings: " I will *bless* you, and make your name great, so that you will be a *blessing*. I will *bless* those who *bless* you, and him who curses you I will curse; and by you all the families of the earth will *bless* themselves [or, " be *blessed* "] " (Gen. 12:2-3).

" Blessing " is the communication from one person to another of a relationship and the power of the relationship. When Isaac blessed Jacob, albeit not knowing that it was Jacob (Gen. 27:18-29), he was giving him the inheritance of goods, of happiness, and of the promise of God. What belonged to Isaac, the promise that God had given Abraham, now belonged to Jacob. A current of relationship — almost like a current of electricity — passed between the two, and the blessing was transferred to Jacob.

The same thing on a grander scale is seen in this blessing of Abraham by Yahweh. When Yahweh blesses, man is blessed indeed. Yahweh establishes his own relationship of love with us. "I will bless you, and make your name great." Through the promise to the patriarchs, Israel receives Yahweh's blessing, which is the seal of his promises to provide a land to maintain the inheritance of his people. Through the blessing, Israel receives assurance that Yahweh's grace will be faithful. In blessing Israel, Yahweh gives himself to her. "You shall be my people, and I will be your God." The divine life has entered into Israel's life. God is with her.

If we stopped there, or if Israel had stopped there, we would have nothing but a cozy clique with God, something like that sentimental old song "In the Garden," which pictures the individual walking among the roses alone with Christ. But this is far from the blessing that God gives. We are seldom, if ever, alone with God — "just the two of us." "I will bless you, and make your name great," says Yahweh, "*so that you will be a blessing.*" That we are blessed means, not that we may sit and enjoy an intimate chat with God, but that we are sent forth into the world to be a blessing. The blessing of God is not kept in a box, to be taken out and looked at in private. God blesses so that his blessing may go on beyond ourselves.

Because of Abraham's blessing, Israel is the agent through whom God will bless. "I will bless those who bless you, and him who curses you I will curse." Perhaps it is significant that "those who bless" Abraham are in the plural, and "him who curses" is in the singular. The promise of blessing will fall on deaf ears. The offering of God's love will meet hearts of stone. But Israel hopes that those who refuse God's blessing will be few, and those who joyfully respond will be many.

However men respond, it is Israel's business to be the channel through which God's gift of delivering love is to flow to all men.

At least, Israel hopes that this will mean all men. " By you all the families of the earth will bless themselves." The translation is accurate, but the verb admits another equally good rendering: " By you [or " through you "] all the families of the earth will be blessed." Abraham and the nation of his descendants are the means by which mankind is to enter into God's love.

We hear a great deal about the narrowness of the Old Testament God and the universality of the God of the New Testament. Let no one affirm this if he reads the promise to Abraham! The New Testament has no new God. His universality is presumed by Israel, not consistently but insistently. Israel makes no claim to exclusive possession of God. Rather, she claims that she is possessed exclusively by God. But this is not the pride of position. It is the acknowledgment of servitude. Perhaps at times Israel has drawn in upon herself, has hedged God around with her assertion that she is the chosen people. But in Abraham, Israel is the nucleus of humanity. The relationship between man and God revolves around the covenant with God's own people.

Obedience and faithfulness will demonstrate to mankind that God has taken a hand in man's life. Israel is to point not to herself but to the God of her history. Her faithfulness to the covenant God is the message of deliverance. " By you all the families of the earth will be blessed."

LEGEND AND HISTORY

We have seen previously that the historic facts of this ancient memory are obscured by the veils of time. To seek for the portraits of Abraham, Isaac, Jacob, and Joseph is to follow a will-o'-the-wisp that must always elude us. We can see the patriarchs only through the eyes of Israel. And Israel was more interested in their significance than in their biographies or their personalities. With Gen., chs. 12 to 50, we are dealing with legend. The legend has some basis in history, of course, but we shall find it less than we might wish. We should also repeat what has been said before: much of the material on the patriarchs, and particularly on Jacob's children, is tribal memory, not the memory of individuals. Exactly how much we cannot know.

Let us begin with the figure whom we can pinpoint in history with the most confidence, Joseph. Although the story of Joseph's being sold into slavery probably represents the descent of the Joseph tribes into Egypt, the story of Joseph's rise to power in Egypt may have a basis in fact. Most scholars feel that this would have been most likely in the years from about 1720 to 1550 B.C., when Egypt was ruled by a heterogeneous group of non-Egyptian invaders known as the Hyksos. In that period nothing would be strange about a Hebrew's rise to the post of prime minister of Egypt. Then the " new king . . . who did not know Joseph " (Ex. 1:8) would mean the return of a native Egyptian dynasty to power in about 1550 B.C. But since we can be sure that the oppression of Israel narrated in Ex., ch. 1, took place about 1300 B.C., some two hundred and fifty years have been compressed into one verse, Ex. 1:8. A better possibility is suggested by other scholars. When Joseph is given the daughter of the high priest of On in marriage (Gen. 41:45), it is clearly a very great honor. Now the priesthood of On was of no political importance in the Hyksos period. But it had great influence at the time of Ikhnaton (1369–1353 B.C.). Furthermore, the rise of a foreigner to power in Egypt is quite typical of the rather casual way in which Ikhnaton ran his kingdom. He was more interested in his religious reforms than in his political responsibilities. After his death, the representatives of rival religious groups regained enough power to eradicate Ikhnaton's religious and political heresies. So the time after Ikhnaton represents the best time for the "new king . . . who did not know Joseph." We may be fairly certain, therefore, that the Joseph tribes went to Egypt between about 1400 and 1360 B.C.

As for Jacob, we can probably presume that the memory of his movements comes from a time before that of Joseph. This would be true at least of Jacob's sojourn in Paddan-aram with the Aramean Laban, and of his travels in central Palestine. These probably represent nomadic tribal movements from as early as 1600 to 1450 or so. But Jacob's stories also include the conflicts with Esau, which take place mainly in Transjordan. (Gen. 32:1 to 33:17.) Esau is Edom, and the Jacob-Esau stories probably represent the struggles of some tribes related to Jacob to establish themselves in Transjordan. The Edomites arrived in Transjordan, as archaeology shows us, about 1300. The memories of long-past tribal movements have been combined in the Jacob story into what looks like a straightforward personal narrative.

The Isaac stories seem to present a serious inconsistency of dates. If Isaac came before Jacob, he must be dated around 1600 B.C. But the only important things Isaac did are in connection with the Philistines. (Gen., ch. 26.) The Philistines did not arrive in Palestine until after 1180 B.C. So the connections between Isaac and the Philistines have simply been written off as anachronisms. Yet we may not dismiss them so easily. To be sure, the Philistines later occupied territory around the shrine in Beer-sheba, where the Isaac stories were presumably transmitted. But there seems to be no compelling reason to deny that Isaac lived after the Philistine invasion. To date him after 1180 B.C., of course, is to doubt that Isaac was the son of

Abraham and the father of Jacob.

We saw in Chapter 2 something of the process through which the Abraham story grew into its present form. What can we say of Abraham in history? The travels of Abraham, like those of Jacob, probably represent tribal travels. The location of his origin in "Ur of the Chaldeans" (Gen. 11:28, 31), however, seems to be a detail that finds its best explanation in the exile. Since many of the people of Israel were in Babylonia (then ruled for the first time by the Chaldeans), the tradition arose that Abraham, the covenantal father, had also come from Babylonia in a prefiguration of their own hoped-for return.

But Abraham is the first man in the Old Testament who is referred to as a "Hebrew" (Gen. 14:13) — an epithet that the Israelites never used for themselves. When it is used in the Old Testament, it is either spoken by non-Israelites or used by Israelites in speaking to foreigners. It is a matter of scholarly debate whether the Israelites are to be connected with a people called the "Habirū," or sometimes "'Apirū," who were to be found all over the ancient Near East. The Habirū were groups of marauding soldiers of fortune who were spread from Babylonia to Egypt during most of the second millennium B.C. They are prominently mentioned in a group of letters (called the *Tell el-Amarna* letters) from Canaanite princes to the Egyptian monarchs Amenhotep III and Amenhotep IV (our old friend Ikhnaton), from about 1410 to 1360 B.C. The letters are requests to Egypt for help against invading bands of Habirū. A good deal of Habirū activity is reflected in these letters in the southern part of Palestine, particularly around the cities of Jerusalem, Bethlehem, Gezer, Lachish, and Hebron. Scholars have debated vigorously for years on the relation of the Hebrews to the Habirū. The author of this book thinks that there was a connection, that the Israelites came from groups of Habirū. Abraham, " the Hebrew," spent most of his time in Hebron, which was a center of Habirū invasions. So it seems quite probable that Abraham's movements are to be dated about the time of the *Tell el-Amarna* letters, at some time, that is, between 1400 and 1350 B.C.

Thus we have the following possible reconstruction of the history behind the patriarchal legends:

1. Jacob tribes came into central Palestine perhaps about 1500.
2. Some trouble in and around Shechem (Gen., chs. 34 and 37:12-24) caused the Joseph tribes to be expelled from central Palestine. They, perhaps with the tribe of Levi, went to Egypt around 1400 B.C. or a little later.
3. One of their number (whether originally named Joseph or not) rose to power in the reign of Ikhnaton (1369–1353 B.C.).
4. At about the same time, between 1400 and 1350 B.C., some tribes among the Habirū were invading and settling in southern Palestine. This is reflected in the Abraham stories. Other tribes were moving into the extreme north of Palestine.
5. Some tribes, probably related to the Jacob tribes of central Palestine, may have moved out to Transjordan, where they encountered resistance from the incoming Edomites, about 1300 B.C.
6. The rise of a new dynasty not long after the death of Ikhnaton caused oppression on the Joseph tribes who were in Egypt, and they, along with the tribe of Levi, formed the group that was in the exodus, about 1290 B.C.
7. Isaac lived well after the conquest of Canaan under Joshua and the tribes of the exodus, and after the Philistine invasion, which was in 1180–1175 B.C.

What has happened, of course, is that the stories have been told and retold, polished, embellished, and combined over many long centuries. When the priestly writers after the exile sought to give form to Israel's tradition, they provided the links among the patriarchs and put the Abraham, Isaac, and Jacob traditions into the order in which we now have them. The tales were so old by then that no one knew the facts of the matter, and no one particularly cared. The important thing was — and is — what the stories say to Israel of God.

What they say is that Yahweh is a God who keeps his promises. He is our God and we are his people. He has chosen his own. Israel did not try to explain why God had chosen Abraham, Isaac, and Jacob any more than they tried to explain why he had chosen the nation Israel. Indeed, we may sometimes wonder at God's poor taste as we read the tales of these ancient characters. Abraham is the man of great faith, but he lies to people about his wife in order to save his skin, and he is harsh with the mother of his son Ishmael when Sarah's feminine jealousy pricks at him. Jacob is "Israel" herself, but he is one of the shrewdest and most unscrupulous rascals in literature, buying his brother's birthright and stealing his blessing, bilking his father-in-law out of his wealth by unorthodox (and impossible) breeding methods (Gen. 30:25-43), and seeking to buy Esau's good will by presents (ch. 32:3-21). Sometimes, as one theologian has put it, "God chooses those who are not particularly choice." But God is faithful. The unfaithfulness and perversity of man does not alter God's intentions. He has chosen Israel to be the nation of his purpose, and he has given them the land, the descendants, and the blessing. The fulfillment of that blessing, however, lies in the future. "If you are Christ's, then you are Abraham's offspring, heirs according to promise." (Gal. 3:29.)

CHAPTER 6 | *"In the Beginning"*

A MYTH, we said in Chapter 2, is a story that reveals man's awareness of himself in relation to his world. It is by means of myth that man expresses his most profound thought. To raise the question of myth's truth, therefore, is to raise at once the wrong question and the right one. Myth is not true if by truth you mean that which is exactly in accord with facts. Adam and Eve are not historical as Moses is. But myth is most profoundly true if by truth you mean that which tells you accurately who and what you are. We can perhaps recognize ourselves more clearly in Adam and Eve than we can in Moses. This is the intention of myth: to hold up a mirror to the reader.

Thus far in our discussion of the Pentateuch, we have seen how Israel described herself *as Israel*. Israelite man is man under the covenant. He is a "peculiar treasure" (Ex. 19:5, KJV). The first eleven chapters of Genesis have to do much less with Israelite man than with man *simply as man*. What is that humanity to whom Israel must mediate God's love? What is the condition of man to which the covenant history is the answer?

GOD AND THE WORLD

The first fact about man is that he is the creature of God. This is not an unusual human viewpoint. Almost every peo-

ple in the world's history has assumed that a God or gods created man and the world. Indeed, the Creation stories in Gen.,
chs. 1 and 2, have echoes from creation myths of other cultures. But like most customs and ideas that Israel borrowed,
these have undergone a change in the transfer. The picture of
man in the Creation is a characteristically Israelite one.

We have, in Gen., chs. 1 and 2, not one but two stories of
creation. One goes from ch 1:1 to the first half of ch. 2:4. The
other begins with the words " In the day " in ch. 2:4 and continues to the end of the chapter. The stories are quite different.
The first is a priestly story; the second, a much earlier one.
The first uses the term " God "; the second, " Yahweh God "
(in English, " the Lord God "). The first has the familiar
seven-day structure; the second has no time reference. God
creates by speaking in ch. 1, but in ch. 2 he works with his
hands, forming man and the animals (the verb is the one used
of a potter " forming " a pot). In ch. 1 man and woman are
created last of all, but in ch. 2 man is the first of creation and
woman last. And ch. 2 has the Garden of Eden, but ch. 1 does
not. These are a few of the differences, enough to show that
the Hebrews were speaking of creation not in scientific but in
religious terms. The " science versus religion " controversy has
no support in the Old Testament idea of creation.

The priestly Creation account makes two points: man is the
crown and climax of God's creation, and worship is built into
the order of things. " In the beginning God created the heavens and the earth. The earth was without form and void." The
process of creation is a bringing of order out of chaos. The
Hebrews seem to have felt that God had the raw material at
hand. This is even clearer in an alternative and equally accurate translation of the beginning of ch. 1: " When God began
to create the heavens and the earth, then the earth was form-
less and empty." The process moves from one stage to the

next. In the first three days God sets the stage. Light, the firmament of heaven, the earth, the seas, and plants are set in order by his word (vs. 3-13). We cannot be sure what picture of the universe the writers had in mind. It may have been something like this:

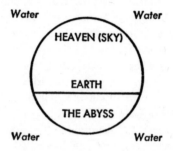

In the second three days of creation, God puts the inhabitants in his universe. The sun, moon, and stars inhabit the sky, the birds fly across it, water creatures live in the sea, and animals live on the earth. And finally God comes to the point. "Let us make man in our image, after our likeness; and let them have dominion over the fish of the sea, and over the birds of the air, and over the cattle, and over all the earth, and over every creeping thing that creeps upon the earth." (V. 26.) To man is given the responsibility of ruling the creation. In this way he is to be "in the image of God." His dominion is the reflection of God's dominion. Man is to see that the order that God brought out of chaos is maintained. He is blessed with fruitfulness, and his business is to enhance the goodness and fruitfulness of God's nature.

When God had finished and had seen that everything "was very good," he rested. Here is the reason for the six days of creation. There are six days because God rested on the seventh. Israel's pattern of worship is built into the order of creation. (See Ex. 20:8-11.) One day in seven (for Israel the last day of the week) is God's day. Christians observe the first day of the week, " the Lord's Day," not because they have rejected the Sabbath but because they worship on the day that Christ rose from the dead and re-created man in God's eyes by redemption. The work of Christ, which makes us " a new creation " (II Cor. 5:17), is the focus of our worship.

In the second Creation story, man emerges at the beginning of the work. Nothing is there but the " mist " over the face of the ground. An echo of the Babylonian creation story is here:

" When on high the heaven had not been named,
Firm ground below had not been called by name,
Naught but primordial Apsu, their begetter,
(And) Mummu-Tiamat, she who bore them all,
Their waters commingling as a single body."

The " commingling " of the subterranean waters (Apsu) and of the ocean waters (Mummu-Tiamat) is the same as the " mist " (Gen. 2:6). Then Yahweh makes man from dust. This too is similar to Mesopotamian ideas of man. In one of the great epics of Babylonia (the Gilgamesh epic), we are told that one of the goddesses " pinched off clay " to create a great hero. Yet there is a difference. Mesopotamian man was viewed as little more than clay, a little figurine who could be manipulated at will by the gods. Hebrew man saw himself as given dignity by God. For God " formed man of dust from the ground, and breathed into his nostrils the breath of life; and man became a living being " (or " living soul "). Man is dust, a creature like the other creatures. But he is given the " breath of life." God himself breathes life into man, and man can properly be called " a living soul " (KJV). Man does not *have* a soul; he *is* a soul. The Hebrew never divides man into body and soul. The physical and spiritual are never radically separated. Man cannot be man without both.

As in the first Creation story, man has a responsibility. He is put into the Garden of Eden (which may mean "the garden of delight") "to till it and keep it." But something is not yet right. Man is not complete. "It is not good that the man should be alone; I will make him a helper fit for him." (Ch. 2:18.) God seems in this story to be working almost by trial and error. He brings the animals to man. But man cannot have the right relationship with them; they are not "fit," or, as we might translate ch. 2:20, "there was not found a helper as standing face to face with him." The answer must be in man himself. The idea of the creation of woman from man's rib is probably quite as old as is male-dominated society. And when Yahweh presents this bewitching creature to the man, he does what men have been doing ever since: he breaks into poetry.

> "This at last is bone of my bones
>   and flesh of my flesh;
>   she shall be called Woman [*ishshah*]
>   because she was taken out of Man [*ish*]."
>   (Ch. 2:23.)

Man is complete. He has now become a human being, for he stands in the society of his own. The fundamental character of man is relationship. And in the relationship of love, man and woman become "one flesh."

WHAT HAVE YOU DONE?

A second fact about man is clear in these chapters. Though he is the creature of God, man becomes a sinner. Though he is made to be God's servant, he prefers to serve himself. Self is at the center of sin. And the various myths that illustrate man's sin are really variations on a theme rather than a picture of sin's development. The theme is man's attempt to make himself " like God." Herein lies the human problem. The variations show the different ways in which we put ourselves at the center of things.

Sin is self-idolatry. This basic fact about sin is rehearsed for us in Gen., ch. 3. The man had been given a command: " You may freely eat of every tree of the garden; but of the tree of the knowledge of good and evil you shall not eat, for in the day that you eat of it you shall die " (ch. 2:16-17). But the snake was subtle. And his blandishments persuaded the woman to eat of the fruit of that forbidden tree.

What is wrong with eating it? Is not " the knowledge of good and evil " something we ought to have? Clearly it is not. The knowledge of good and evil is a knowledge that belongs only to God. " God knows that when you eat of it your eyes will be opened, and you will be like God, knowing good and evil." (Ch. 3:5.) In a religion that puts so much emphasis on morality, the forbidden knowledge cannot be the ability to make moral distinctions. Rather, this knowledge is controlling knowledge, and " good and evil " here means anything that happens to man, from the most pleasant to the most unpleasant. The " knowledge of good and evil," therefore, is the ability to control what will happen to us. But this God alone can do, and for this we must simply trust God. In the effort to be " master of our fate," we are seeking to be " like God." We are seeking a way out of the necessity of trusting God.

And the snake's prediction is true. " Your eyes will be opened," he had promised. " Then the eyes of both were opened," and they saw — not that they were divine but that they were naked! The irony of man's pretensions to divinity rings loud. Man cannot achieve divinity. If he fails to trust God, he realizes only his own helplessness. And when God himself comes, man flees in terror (ch. 3:8), cowering in the deepest thicket he can find. Man the master, man the heir to

God's own power, man the ruler of creation, at the moment of his highest self-idolatry is reduced to a cowardly, trembling, naked soul, helpless and afraid.

Yet his illusion of divinity does not desert him. "Who told you that you were naked?" God asks. And the first instance of "passing the buck" occurs. Man can blame not only the woman but, slyly, God himself. "The woman whom *thou gavest* to be with me, she gave me fruit of the tree." The woman in her turn blames the serpent, and the serpent, having no one else to blame, can only lie low.

Then comes the curse. (Vs. 14-19.) The harmony between man and nature is ended, and they become deadly enemies. Human society is shattered. Whereas before it was a partnership in which the two were one, now it is dominated by the man. The outcome of love in childbirth is pain, and the overwhelming desire of woman remains at the mercy of her husband. He is the boss. And man's fulfillment of his function is threatened. The soil (Hebrew, *'ādāmāh*) from which man (*'ādām*) was taken turns un-co-operative; work becomes toil, and death the punishment for a life of unremitting sweat. "You shall surely die," God had said. Death ceases to be the normal order and becomes the culmination of man's punishment. He may no longer eat of the "tree of life," lest he extend his monstrous illusion indefinitely. (Vs. 22-24.) Sin has become the stage on which life is played. Man, trying to be God, has become less than true man.

Sin is self-isolation. In the Cain and Abel story we have a common theme of rivalry between the shepherd (Abel) and the farmer (Cain). But this is not the principal issue. The point comes in Cain's attitude. When Abel's sacrifice is accepted and Cain's is not, Cain becomes angry. The storytellers do not tell us why Yahweh does not accept Cain's offering. It does not matter. For Cain has no reason to be angry. "If you

do well," Yahweh says, " will you not be accepted? " Perhaps
Cain depends too much on sacrifice to keep him in God's good
graces. Acceptance depends, rather, on his " doing well." Yet
this is the most difficult relationship to maintain. We can never
be certain that we are doing well, and we *can* be certain that
we are sacrificing properly. But the goal of faith is not certainty; rather, it is the mastering of sin, which waits to
pounce like an animal in ambush (ch. 4:7).

But Cain is unable to master sin. Like a petulant child, he
" takes it out " on his younger brother. Man's anger at God is
displayed in the breaking of his human relationships. Cain has
rejected his responsibility. " Am I my brother's keeper? " He
has not only rejected Yahweh's exhortation to do well; he has
shut himself away within himself, refusing to recognize that
he cannot be isolated. " No man is an Iland, intire of it selfe,"
wrote John Donne. And when we seek to insulate ourselves
(literally, make ourselves islands), we have ceased to be man
as man properly is. We become, like Cain, " fugitives and wanderers on the earth " (v. 12). Our failure to exercise responsibility toward our fellows makes us suspicious that they will
do the same. We flee from them and wander in the vacuum of
our own self-isolation.

The " song of Lamech " (vs. 23-24) illustrates this further.
Our insulation against others gives us a savage joy when we
strike out against them.

> " If Cain is avenged sevenfold,
>   truly Lamech seventy-sevenfold."

Relationship turns into revenge. The family of man is split
asunder.

Sin is self-elevation. If there is one thing on which the Old
Testament is emphatic, it is that man is not God. There is no
" spark of the divine " in man. He is man, and man he must

remain. Indeed, his trouble arises in his attempt to usurp divinity to himself. Man must trust God to be God, and if he does not, he has confused the world's order.

But men do not seem to learn. A very strange little myth is the one in Gen. 6:1-4, where the "sons of God" marry the daughters of men. This is clearly a remnant from the belief in many gods (polytheism). But it is here probably because it illustrates again man's willingness to seek divinity. To be sure, the "sons of God" are primarily responsible. But the offspring of these unnatural marriages are apparently becoming too healthy. They are the "mighty men." We probably do not have the whole story, but it gives rise to God's decision to limit the span of man's life to one hundred and twenty years. Man's long life might again give him delusions of divinity.

Even this does not solve the problem. "Yahweh saw that the wickedness of man was great in the earth, and that every imagination of the thoughts of his heart was only evil continually." (V. 5.) A strong statement it is, and the response is equally drastic. The Flood wipes out life, and God starts over again. (The Flood stories are doubtless adapted from part of the Babylonian Gilgamesh epic.) God's first trial has seemingly failed.

Sin is self-congratulation. God's next attempt fails too. No sooner has Noah returned to dry ground than he plants a vineyard and gets drunk on its produce. (Ch. 9:20-21.) When his son Ham sees him naked in his drunken stupor, he tells his brothers. We can fairly see him giggling over his father's helpless state. But Noah's curse comes not on Ham but on Ham's son, Canaan. Of course, it was the Canaanites in particular with whom the Hebrews had to contend. And where the Canaanites worshiped Baal, whom they could control with magic, the Israelites worshiped the invisible Yahweh, who could not be controlled. The Canaanites could see the external weakness

of Hebrew faith, and they could congratulate themselves on it.
Is this not also our case? We too congratulate ourselves on
viewing the faults of others. " I am safe," we think. Yet sud-
denly the withering of our arrogance comes upon us. " Let any
one who thinks that he stands," says Paul, " take heed lest he
fall." (I Cor. 10:12.)

Sin is self-preservation. " Now the whole earth had one language and few words." (Gen. 11:1.) The myth of the Tower of
Babel probably began as the explanation of man's many languages. This is still part of its purpose, but a larger point can
be seen. Men build cities and civilizations for themselves. But
men are prone to eye their accomplishments as nothing less
than their salvation. " Come, let us build ourselves a city, and
a tower with its top in the heavens, and let us make a name for
ourselves, lest we be scattered abroad upon the face of the
whole earth." (V. 4.)

The Tower of Babel is usually understood to be the great
Temple of Marduk in the city of Babylon (Hebrew, *bābel*).
Etemenanki was its name, " the House of the Foundation
Platform of Heaven and Earth." Babylonian temples were
built as stepped towers (ziggurats, they were called), with the
shrine on the very top. Yet the word by which this tower is
designated is Migdol, a word that never speaks elsewhere of a
temple-tower but only of defense towers, battlements. The
building of the tower is a kind of " storming of the gates of
heaven," but it is a strangely defensive assault. Man seeks by
this means to preserve himself, to gain his immortality
(" make a name ") by his technical prowess, to assure his
safety, " lest we be scattered abroad."

But this attempt by man to secure his own defense over
against God is an affront to Yahweh. " This is only the beginning of what they will do; and nothing that they propose to
do will now be impossible for them." (V. 6.) If man can suc-

ceed in isolating himself from God by the fortresses of his own making, his delusions of divinity will not be hindered. So God does what men feared: he scatters them abroad by confusing their language. Men can no longer understand each other. Human communication breaks down when man tries to ascend to heights where he does not belong.

The relationship of this story with Babylon is perhaps a secondary one. The words "Babel" and "confuse" (*bālal*) are not in any way related. But when Israel was in exile, Babylon was the focus of her frustration. The great city must have seemed the very center of confusion and idolatry. And so it has always seemed to Israel. Even in the New Testament, Babylon is the great harlot who exalts herself against God. (Rev., chs. 17 and 18.)

It seems a grim picture that we have drawn. Man, the creature of God, persists in seeking to replace God with himself. He goes from sin to sin, from self-idolatry to self-idolatry, from bad to worse. Is there nothing good to be said of man? Christians are sometimes accused of dragging man in the dirt with their ideas of sin. But sin is not the last word. Christians are the most realistic and hopeful of men. For we know, as the Old Testament knows, that God has mercy on man.

INTIMATIONS OF MERCY

It seems that God never leaves men completely to their own devices. Even when men try to get out from under God's rule, even when they defy him and shout "No!" to his face, his love preserves them. Mercy always comes upon men in the very midst of their sin. Adam and Eve have no sooner heard the curse than their nakedness is clothed by God himself (Gen. 3:21). Cain has no sooner heard his sentence to wander than he receives the mark that will preserve him from murder (ch. 4:14-15). So God acts. He cares for men at the height of their sin, as we have seen in the stories of the wilderness wandering. The love of God is his covenant love, steadfast and faithful. Punishment itself is an act of love. For love seeks not the gratification of the other but seeks the greatest good for the other.

God has created man, not so that he might have someone on whom to vent his wrath, but so that he might manifest his love. If man persists in corrupting God's good gift through his self-idolatry, God does not simply take away the gift. Rather, he seeks to teach us how to use it. Though he determined to put an end to man on the earth, yet " Noah found favor in the eyes of Yahweh " (ch. 6:8). Was this because he was " blameless in his generation " (ch. 6:9 — priestly; ch. 7:1 — probably priestly) ? The remark seems almost offhand. At any rate, the favor that Noah found does not seem to have been based on his righteousness. God's mercy does not depend on our goodness. Indeed, the power of mercy is that it overcomes our evil.

And mercy issues in covenant. God promises never again to destroy man from the earth. " While the earth remains, seedtime and harvest, cold and heat, summer and winter, day and night, shall not cease." (Ch. 8:22.) Though punishment is real and severe, mercy is the last word. When God promises in covenant, his promise is sealed and sure. " Never again shall all flesh be cut off by the waters of a flood, and never again shall there be a flood to destroy the earth." (Ch. 9:11.) When the storms come and rain lashes at the earth, man need not fear the return of the flood. For the rainbow is the evidence that the sun breaks through the clouds. (Vs. 13-16.) There is an end of wrath, and its end is the remembrance of mercy.

But the covenant with Noah points on toward the other covenants that we have discussed. In chs. 1 to 11, the priestly writers have symbolized this by providing the tables of generations. We may pause over them briefly.

THE " BEGATS "

No reader should feel compelled to read every word of the Bible. Many resolute souls who have begun to read it from beginning to end have foundered on the genealogies in Gen., chs. 5, 10, and 11. Perhaps the best advice is to skip them until such time as they can be read with profit and interest. This discussion is aimed at clarifying the reason for which they are here.

The genealogies illustrate the process of selection that we saw in the patriarchal stories. The priestly writers have put them in to show that God began far back in the world's history to work toward the covenant with Israel. The first set of " begats " carries us from Adam to Noah. (Chs. 4:17 to 5:32.) Two sets of genealogies are there: one gives the descendants of Cain, the other those of Seth. As a matter of fact, these two may be variant versions of a single genealogy. Enoch and Lamech occur in both lists. In the Cainite list, Lamech is the son of Methushael; in the Sethite list he is the son of Methuselah. The two names are so similar that they probably began as the same. Furthermore, both Adam and Enosh mean " man." And if we put these two lists in parallel columns, placing Adam and Enosh across from each other, this is the result:

Cainite	*Sethite*
	Seth
Adam	Enosh
Cain (Hebrew *qaín*)	Kenan (Hebrew *qêynān*)
Enoch	Mahalalel
Irad	Jared
Mehujael	Enoch
Methushael	Methuselah
Lamech	Lamech

Cain and Kenan are different spellings of the same name, as
are Irad and Jared, and Mehujael and Mahalalel. The order of
the three names from Enoch to Mehujael in the Cainite list
has been reversed in the Sethite one. The Cainite list does not
carry on to Noah but to those founders of civilization, Jabal
(the father of nomads), Jubal (the father of musicians), and
Tubal-cain (the father of industrialists).

Questions have been raised about the great ages of these
ancient characters. The shortest life in ch. 5 is Lamech's, seven
hundred and seventy-seven years. The reason their lives are
said to be so long rests on the fact that every age longs for
" the good old days." The distant past always seems in some
way better than the present. Add to that the Hebraic assump-
tion that the good life is the long life. The ancient patriarchs
lived so long because they lived so long ago, when the world
was thought to be happy and good. A parallel occurs in an
ancient Sumerian king list. Legendary kings of the past
reigned for unbelievable times: one Alulimak, for example,
is said to have ruled for 28,800 years! Alalgar was king for
36,000 years! But Enmenuanlak topped them all; he reigned
for 43,200 years. We can only admire the Hebrews' restraint.

In ch. 10, the effort is made to show how all the peoples of
the earth were descended from Noah's sons, Shem, Ham, and
Japheth. Japheth's sons are mostly peoples of Asia Minor and
the eastern Mediterranean area (Javan, for example, denotes
the Greeks). The sons of Ham are mainly African and southern Arabian, except for Canaan. But it is with the sons of
Shem that the priestly writers clarify their purpose. (Vs. 21-
31.) They first list Shem's sons, then the sons of Aram (the
Arameans). They then follow Arpachshad through Shelah to
Eber. Eber had two sons, Peleg and Joktan, and this list follows the Arabian descendants of Joktan. But that is not all
they have to tell us. In ch. 11:10-20, the rest of Shem's gene-

alogy is given. Once more we are sent through Arpachshad, Shelah, and Eber. But this time we follow Eber through Peleg. At each point the existence of "other sons and daughters" is mentioned, but we are to be interested in only one. We follow through Peleg's son Reu, his son Serug, and his son Nahor. To Nahor was born Terah. Terah had three sons, Abram, Nahor, and Haran. He took his family to the city which was later named for Haran, but only Abram moved on to the promised land.

So the genealogies are an integral part of the covenant history. Selection takes place generation after generation. And when the "begats" are finished, we have come down to the one elected man, Abraham. The covenant with Israel has been in process, so the genealogies claim, since the beginning of time. If we have eyes to see, even the most uninteresting parts of Scripture can tell us something of God's work in the world.

CHAPTER 7 | *"You Shall Be My People"*

Decision" is an important word in religious discussion.
Evangelists urge their hearers to "make a decision for Christ."
Young people make decisions about vocation, about college,
about marriage. Men decide basically about themselves, the
meanings of their lives, the allegiances and attachments of
their souls. Yet there is a decision that we usually bypass. And
that is God's decision. The Bible insists that we cannot make
decisions without reference to God's primary decision. "You
did not choose me, but I chose you" (John 15:16) was Jesus'
word to his disciples. Some of us object to the preaching of
some evangelists exactly because they omit this central affirmation of the Bible. One seldom hears an evangelist who, in
urging that we make our decisions, is willing to say, "God
has already made the decision; he has chosen." To be sure,
this might complicate the message for the hearers, and it may
be better that they be confronted by the urgent call to commitment. Yet the Bible says from end to end, "It is *God* who
makes the real decision; it is he who has acted to procure our
reconciliation to him." This affirmation stands at the center of
the Torah, as it stands at the center of the whole Scripture.
The Torah is the history of God's decision. It is the story of
God's choice.

89

THE HISTORY OF CHOICE

We have looked at the Pentateuch thus far in reverse order. We began with the exodus and ended with the Creation and its aftermath. In each major tradition we saw the answer to a question. The exodus and Covenant tradition answered the question, Who is Israel? The tradition of the patriarchs answered the question, What is Israel's place in mankind? The Creation and Fall traditions answered the question, What is that mankind to whom Israel is sent? Now we may turn the picture around, so to speak, and look at it as the Pentateuch presents it to us. Or, to switch the comparison, knowing the end of the detective story, we may now begin over again and see how the clues lead to that end.

The story begins and continues with God. But it is not only about God. It is about God in his relationship with men. Man is the crown of the Creation, the creature with whom God has made a special relationship. This relationship will be maintained by God's love and by man's continuing trust and obedience. It is a relationship of covenant, though the Creation stories do not use the term. But we shatter the relationship by our growing preference for ourselves. We do not want very much to trust God, since our mastery over the world is so satisfying to us. We break the covenant of creation; we do not like to be creatures, we prefer to be " like God." Yet we *are* creatures whether we like it or not. We cannot escape our limitations, much as we might wish to. Yet our delusions of divinity lead to the most radical disruptions of our relationships. Somehow we must start all over again. And it is God who does the starting.

A new covenant comes about. Punishment is followed by reconciliation. God promises never again to punish by destruction, and Noah begins the covenant story anew. Mankind grows and expands, is fruitful and multiplies, and fills the earth. Mankind is growing up. Yet men have not learned the lesson. They still isolate themselves defensively from God. Their Towers of Babel are magnificently arrogant structures, "with their tops in the heavens," but they are the work of desperate men, "lest we be scattered abroad." God's mercy seems not to have touched mankind as a whole. Mankind continues its pretensions to greatness.

But all unseen and unknown by the world, another process has been set in motion. It is a narrowing process, a selectivity, which finally comes down to one man. The fruit has become ripe for picking. "Go from your country and your kindred and your father's house." "So Abram went." Before God can reach mankind as a whole, it seems, he must touch one man. And that one man must become a nation. A third covenant is sealed. The first covenant had been simply a statement of man's proper vocation, to care for the creation. The second had been a promise by God that no destruction would again be visited upon the earth. Its sign was the rainbow, a sign that God himself would give. In the third covenant, God promises to keep his people and make them a blessing. And the sign is one that he commands but that men themselves do. The men of Abraham's family are to practice circumcision. By this means, all men will know that they belong to God.

But this covenant is not yet complete. It leads men on by promise, not by fulfillment. The mercy of God will come to mankind through a nation. Selection continues from Abraham to Isaac (not Ishmael) and to Jacob (not Esau). No such selection of Jacob's sons is made. The broadening of one man into a nation takes place in them. With the families of Jacob's sons the fourth covenant is made. "You shall be my people, and I will be your God." The sign of this covenant is the law. By the trust and obedience of a people, all men will know that they are God's. The promise of this covenant is the promise of the presence of God. "For throughout all their journeys the cloud of Yahweh was upon the tabernacle by day, and fire was in it by night, in the sight of all the house of Israel." (Ex. 40:38.) Israel is set upon a road that does not end. They follow it, winding up and down hills, across rivers, to the Land of Canaan, through anarchy to monarchy, from monarchy to exile, from exile to dispersion throughout the world. But everywhere is the tabernacling presence of God. No matter what the circumstance of life, where the Jew is, there is the presence of God. "You shall be my people, and I will be your God." This is the history of God's decision, as the Torah gives it to us.

THE FOUNDATION STONE

All right, you may say, but what does it say about Christianity? Why should we bother to read about the exodus if we can read about the death and resurrection of Christ? Is not Christ "the end of the law" (Rom. 10:4)? Did he not "fulfil the law and the prophets" (Matt. 5:17)? If the fulfillment has come, why go back to the preliminaries? Paul settled it once and for all that Christians did not have to become Jews. What has the Torah to say to the Christian? We celebrate the Lord's Supper, not Passover. We have Baptism, not circumcision.

Perhaps it should be said that one of the earliest Christian heresies was Marcionism, which wanted to do away with the Old Testament entirely. And the church was sometimes hard put to it to discover just why, if there was a New Testament, we should keep the Old. It was sometimes retained as a book of predictions concerning Christ, predictions that were found in the most unlikely places. One example will be sufficient. In Gen. 14:14 is reference to 318 men with Abraham. The

Epistle of Barnabas, a Christian writing of the second century A.D., took the number 318 to be a prophecy of Christ. Eighteen is a combination of 10 and 8. In Greek figuring, 10 was designated by I and 8 by H. These are the first two letters of the Greek spelling of the name Jesus; the 18, therefore, refers to Jesus. And 300 was designated by T, which is the cross. Abraham's 318 men, the epistle presumed, had nothing to do with history but was a hidden prophecy of the cross of Christ.

Of course, such interpretation is too fantastic to be acceptable. But the question remains. What has the Pentateuch to say to the Christian, aside from an occasional verse that contains religious insight? The first thing we must say is that Jesus was a Jew. Let us never forget that. The Torah was Holy Scripture to Jesus. When he stated the two greatest commandments, the first was from Deuteronomy and the second from Leviticus. "If they do not hear Moses and the prophets, neither will they be convinced if some one should rise from the dead" (Luke 16:31) was the "punch line" of one of his parables. The Old Testament is the *necessary* forerunner of Jesus. Someone has gone so far as to say that the New Testament without the Old Testament is not a Christian book. What does that mean? It means that the New Testament does not *replace* the Old but that it *fulfills* the Old. You can no more remove the New Testament from the Old Testament than you can cut a flower from its stalk and claim that it is the whole plant.

The Torah tells us of God's action. It gives us the principle that God's gracious acts in history lead on to the covenant that applies to mankind. Yet how is mankind to receive the covenant? Israel could never find the answer. We cannot doubt that her covenant with God was a real relationship. God's action in the exodus was the action of the same God whom we worship. But the action was not complete. The covenant did not apply to all mankind. Another action was necessary if the first was to be completed. Christians find that action in the life, death, and resurrection of Christ. Christ came not merely to teach us about the good life but to live out the event in history through which mankind could become the children of the covenant. It is a new covenant, yet it is not fundamentally different from the old. It is brought into being by God's action, and it is sealed by our response, just as was Israel's covenant.

The Torah tells us likewise of God's requirement. We belong to him. Every facet of life must be directed to his purpose. Halfhearted faithfulness is no faithfulness at all. "You shall love Yahweh your God with all your heart, and with all your soul, and with all your might." (Deut. 6:5.) But the law is incomplete. The law tends to become a stick that we can hold over God's head: "Look, I have been obedient. Now reward me!" This is not trust but legalism. But in Christ our trust is in a person. "The Word became flesh and dwelt among us, full of grace and truth; we have beheld his glory." (John 1:14.) We no longer obey law on tables of stone or on paper. We obey the Person who has reconciled us to God. And in obeying him, we believe, we are obeying God himself. As our Lord insisted, this does not "abolish the law and the prophets." It fulfills them. It takes life out of allegiance to mere rules and makes it into allegiance to personal love. The rules are now applicable as guides to the life of love.

The Torah tells us finally of God's people. Men are not related to God in isolation from other men. On the contrary, the relationship with God immediately involves relationship with other men. The love of God leads immediately to the love of the neighbor. And the two cannot be separated. Just as we saw how Abraham emerged in God's plan out of mankind in order to form a nation that would be a blessing to "all the families of the earth," so we can see how Christ emerges out of Israel to form a people that will ultimately include all mankind. We sometimes speak of the church, with Paul, as the "Israel of God" (Gal. 6:16), that is, the successor and extension of Israel. But this is true because Christ himself brought Israel to a focus in himself. He underwent an "exodus," a passing from death to life. He himself, if we may say it this way, is the last step in the process of choice. The new covenant in Christ is not a covenant between us and Christ but is a covenant between God and Christ. We become children of the covenant by partaking in Christ's inheritance. (See Rom. 8:14-17.)

And we are a people, a body that has many members but that is a single body. The principle of our existence as a people is now no longer human generation but the rebirth from God himself. Israel too was a body, but the difficulty was that — if so crude an image may be used — the body had no head. Yet from Israel we learn what being the people of God means. It means our solidarity in worship. It means our union in action. It means our mutuality in love.

It also means our fervency in hope. "By you all the families of the earth will be blessed," God said to Abraham. We echo the promise as we preach the gospel of Christ to the families of the earth. But they are not all blessed. The families of the earth are not yet one family; they have not been taken into "the household of God" (Eph. 2:19). And until they are incorporated into that family, our faith remains a hope. In that, we are at one with the Jew. He too looks toward the age of blessedness when mankind will be one, a fitting servant for the God who is One. In the meantime, it is not too much for Christians to say that we need the Jew, that we depend on him. His feet are planted firmly in history, and his stubborn remembrance reminds us not to lift our eyes too far from the common soil of man into the cloudy heavens of speculation. But our expectation is the same. He awaits a coming; we await a " second " coming. Together we will greet the One who comes.

And the book is the same. A Jew, speaking to Christians, said, " To you, the book is a forecourt; to us, it is the sanctuary." But the same God is speaking in it. If for us the word that he speaks is like a sentence unfinished until Christ adds the final phrase, it is nonetheless his word. And if we are true to that word, if we hear it in faithfulness, may we not find ourselves better able to grasp the true word of Christ? Perhaps no one will seem to listen to our word. But we shall await that day when the promise to Abraham is complete, when all the families of the earth are blessed, when the tree of life, which has been barred to us since Adam left the Garden, will be accessible for the healing of the nations.

> " Behold, the dwelling of God is with men. He will dwell with them, and they shall be his people, and God himself will be with them." (Rev. 21 :3.)

FIRST UNITED PRESBYTERIAN CHURCH
2619 BROADWAY
OAKLAND 12, CALIFORNIA